what parents are saying
dunstan baby lang

"Thank you for the opportunity to learn something new about my child. It was a great help and has brought me more insight into the fact that babies aren't just crying . . . they have something to say."

"I'm glad I was able to use this method with my second child. I only wish I'd known about it for my first. It would have made caring for her a lot easier."

"This system is just amazing! My husband still says, 'He is saying "neh"! He's hungry!' He is so excited because he can understand our son now! I am, too!!"

"My partner and I love Dunstan's method. Our relationship is better and our baby is happier."

"My son was pretty relaxed, but knowing the system helped me feel so confident. I think he is such a good baby and happy because of it."

"I would strongly recommend this system to every parent. It makes you feel that you know what you are doing and that you have some control over this little life that you have created."

"Dunstan's method is highly effective and easy to learn. It's well worth the time to help you understand what your baby needs and wants. It makes everyone's life more contented and has had a positive effect on the whole family."

calm
the
crying

AVERY

a member of

PENGUIN GROUP (USA) INC.

NEW YORK

calm

the

crying

◻

The Secret Baby Language
That Reveals the Hidden Meaning
Behind an Infant's Cry

◻

PRISCILLA DUNSTAN

AVERY

Published by the Penguin Group

Penguin Group (USA) Inc., 375 Hudson Street, New York, New York 10014, USA • Penguin Group (Canada), 90 Eglinton Avenue East, Suite 700, Toronto, Ontario M4P 2Y3, Canada (a division of Pearson Penguin Canada Inc.) • Penguin Books Ltd, 80 Strand, London WC2R 0RL, England • Penguin Ireland, 25 St Stephen's Green, Dublin 2, Ireland (a division of Penguin Books Ltd) • Penguin Group (Australia), 250 Camberwell Road, Camberwell, Victoria 3124, Australia (a division of Pearson Australia Group Pty Ltd) • Penguin Books India Pvt Ltd, 11 Community Centre, Panchsheel Park, New Delhi–110 017, India • Penguin Group (NZ), 67 Apollo Drive, Rosedale, North Shore 0632, New Zealand (a division of Pearson New Zealand Ltd) • Penguin Books (South Africa) (Pty) Ltd, 24 Sturdee Avenue, Rosebank, Johannesburg 2196, South Africa

Penguin Books Ltd, Registered Offices: 80 Strand, London WC2R 0RL, England

Most Avery books are available at special quantity discounts for bulk purchase for sales promotions, premiums, fund-raising, and educational needs. Special books or book excerpts also can be created to fit specific needs. For details, write Penguin Group (USA) Inc. Special Markets, 375 Hudson Street, New York, NY 10014.

Library of Congress Cataloging-in-Publication Data

Dunstan, Priscilla.
Calm the crying : the secret baby language that reveals the hidden meaning behind an infant's cry / Priscilla Dunstan.
p.   cm.
ISBN 978-1-58333-469-0
1. Crying in infants.   2. Nonverbal communication in infants.   3. Infants—Care.   I. Title.
BF720.C78D86   2012   2012024964
649'.122—dc23

Printed in the United States of America
1   3   5   7   9   10   8   6   4   2

Book design by Stephanie Huntwork

While the author has made every effort to provide accurate telephone numbers, Internet addresses, and other contact information at the time of publication, neither the publisher nor the author assumes any responsibility for errors, or for changes that occur after publication. Further, the publisher does not have any control over and does not assume any responsibility for author or third-party websites or their content.

Imagine having been heard and understood your whole life,
even from your first breath and sound.

—PRISCILLA DUNSTAN

CONTENTS

PART 1

newborn words

PART 2

6-week words

PART 3

12-week words

FOREWORD

WHEN I FIRST MET Priscilla Dunstan in 2009, I was initially a bit skeptical of this young Australian mother who believed she could understand a baby's cries. However, I soon found her philosophy to be similar to mine. We both believe that education and support for new parents heavily influences the quality of parenting. Priscilla had devoted her career to translating and decoding infant cries in order to allow parents to better understand their needs. Her success was undeniable—she'd even converted Oprah! I was intrigued.

In my 20 years of practicing pediatrics in New York City, I have come to believe that a critical component of successful bonding between mother and newborn is the support that mother receives – from her partner, family, and physician. This emphasis on support for the mother forms part of the founding philosophy of Tribeca Pediatrics and Tribeca Parenting, which support parents through quality pediatric medical care as well as educational support through classes in topics such as breastfeeding, baby massage, and CPR.

Priscilla shares our commitment to supporting new mothers in their journey to bond with their newborns. A lifetime of researching, listening to, translating, and decoding infants' cries resulted in the

Dustan Baby Language, which helps mothers and fathers connect with their baby through better understanding their baby's sounds and thus better meeting his or her needs. Priscilla's work reinforces the bond between parent and child, much as I do in my practice, and I commend her dedication.

Maternal stress and insecurity can often exacerbate such issues such as breastfeeding, colic, sleep, and general well-being. The techniques that Priscilla offers will help a mother feel more confident that she is meeting her infant's needs, easing the stress of caring for a newborn. Priscilla's techniques work for fathers too, providing a tangible means of connection that's sometimes hard to attain at this early stage when so many of a newborn's needs can seemingly only be satisfied by Mom.

Calm the Crying is a very practical "how to" manual. The Dunstan Baby Language is presented in a very straightforward manner, and will be an accessible tool for new moms and dads. I believe this book will be especially valuable for first-time parents and those unsure of how to care for their infant.

Enjoy Calm the Crying—and best wishes on your journey with your newborn. This is an experience like none other, and I wish you and your baby good luck in finding your path together.

Dr. Michel Cohen
New York City, June 2012
Tribeca Pediatrics

the secret language of babies

WOULDN'T IT BE WONDERFUL if you could understand exactly what your crying baby was trying to tell you? *Calm the Crying* is about just that: how to quickly comprehend and calm your baby's crying. You'll learn how to know what your baby needs— and when—simply by listening to her cries.

Healthy human babies have a universal "secret baby language" based on physical reflexes that all infants share, regardless of nationality or ethnicity. This book uses the Dunstan Classification of Infant Cries to teach you how to listen to your baby from birth and understand the underlying issue that's causing your baby to cry. Through simple explanations that tie specific sounds in crying to phonetic "words," I'll show you how to interpret your baby's cries as easily as if he were speaking your own language. Your baby will literally tell you if she is hungry, tired, needs to burp, feels cold, or has gas. Your baby can even communicate that he's feeling overwhelmed or that his gums are hurting from teething. You will *hear, understand,* and *know* exactly what your baby needs and how to attend to those needs quickly and effectively.

Parents have a deep desire to soothe their little one's distress, feeling helpless and discouraged by a continually crying baby. This book will help you view crying not as a problem but as an opportunity to bond with your baby, because you'll be able to connect your baby's cries to specific needs and respond to them.

This classification method is based on more than thirteen years of research, has been studied in many international independent studies, is taught in more than thirty countries by nurses, pediatricians, and other health workers, and has helped an estimated million-plus babies and their parents. It eliminates much of the frustration, guesswork, and trial and error most parents use when trying to soothe their babies.

Countless parents worldwide have told me (and independent research has shown) that learning their baby's cues has changed their lives, reduced their stress, built their confidence as parents, and deepened their bonds with their baby. Dads find they enjoy caring for their babies now that they can read and respond to their cues. For them, this system is a little like the GPS on a car—it helps them take the most direct route to get where they and their babies need to go. Busy working parents can make the most of their special time with their baby. Grandparents and other relatives can use this system to get quickly in sync with the newest member of the family—and so can your baby's siblings and caregivers. Last but certainly not least, the whole family will likely get more sleep!

Starting with three key "words" babies use as newborns, you'll learn more than ten words babies say in their cries, with detailed descriptions of what the words sound like, how they are made, and what to do when you hear them.

As you practice with your baby, you'll start feeling more and more confident that you know what your baby is telling you. Once the crying is calmed, you can tune in to your baby's daily rhythms and natural patterns and begin to shape a routine that will work for every-one in the family. Sometimes the best routine for your family requires some adjustment on the part of your baby—and a baby who is happy and contented is much more likely to adjust than one who is tired, hungry, and upset. (That goes for grown-ups, too!)

It's also easier to bond and connect with a baby who isn't crying. By calming the crying, you make more time for bonding. There's no better feeling than knowing that you are giving your baby the best possible gift: the security of being heard and understood.

how i discovered the secret language of babies

I WAS BORN being able to hear more than most people, and with exceptional skills in pattern recognition. My mother, who was a music teacher, played music to me in the womb, and I was taken to sym-phony concerts at an early age. At age two, I became obsessed with learning to play the violin. My parents, both educators, encouraged my enthusiasm.

Since my musical capacity grew much faster than my ability to read music at such a young age, my mother would sing or play music on the piano, and I would play the notes back on my violin. It turned out that I could play a concerto back exactly, after hearing it only once. This was how it was discovered that I had an eidetic, or photo-graphic, memory.

My talent for pattern recognition was even greater: once I heard the music of specific composers, I could generally estimate where the music would go or what direction an instrument part would take.

There were some downsides to my abilities. I was often confused when people's words didn't match the emotion in their voice—it was clear to me that their words were saying one thing but their voice was saying another! And my acute hearing was often misunderstood: some found it hard to believe that I heard the sounds I did.

From violin, I moved into classical and operatic singing. I learned the bel canto method, which focuses on the body as an instrument. Singers use it to create that perfect note that brings listeners to tears, fills an opera house without microphones, or breaks a glass. I learned from professionals how tightening one muscle would change the resulting sound. I was fascinated by the impact a large meal could have on sound, or how a tone changes depending on our mental state—for example, what boyfriend trouble would do to the pulse in a girlfriend's voice: it would increase, becoming faster, and the pitch would become higher.

Finally, I began to understand what I had been hearing in peoples' voices all my life. There were *reasons* for what I heard, and what I was hearing was *real*.

The best way to describe how I hear is to use the analogy of a symphony. Where most people hear a violin soloist playing, in that single instrument's sound I hear a symphony of sound: many different tones and parts. When I hear someone speaking, I hear the words and how they're spoken in terms of speed or pitch. I also hear how their body's reactions affect their voice. When we lie, our pulse rate increases, our heart races, and our mouth becomes dryer. These changes make our voice harsher and dryer. If we feel upset or anxious, the tonal pulse rate in our voice increases. If someone has been frightened, I will hear harmonic "holes" in their voice. This information can stay in a voice for days, sometimes longer. I've found that the voice holds up to three days' worth of information (which is why professional opera singers are very guarded about their actions and influences before a concert).

All of this primed me to be highly sensitive to my son's cries when he was born. Also, as the youngest of six children, I had spent my childhood listening to my noisy, talkative family but not feeling heard. When Tom was born, it was very important to me that my son *be heard*.

My auditory ability and training led me to assume that Tom's crying meant something—but for the life of me I couldn't understand what! And he cried *a lot*. I had no idea why he would be screaming one moment and calm the next; why he would sleep for short bursts of five or ten minutes and then wake screaming; why it seemed like nothing I did helped. I felt demoralized that I, his own mother, couldn't seem to meet his needs effectively enough to stop his crying.

A lactation nurse told me Tom had colic. She assured me that I would soon come to know his cries and understand what he wanted.

I asked what I should listen for, and how I could tell the cries apart, but no one could give me an answer. I bought every book on crying I could find, but they didn't tell me how to understand and differentiate between my baby's cries. Graphs, decibel readings, and sound waves aren't much use to a parent desperately trying to soothe an inconsolable baby.

I vividly recall the first, small step that led to my breakthrough. It was about 3:00 a.m. after a particularly hard few days, and Tom had again woken crying. I knew it was going to be a good hour or so before he would stop. I tried everything I could think of, and still he cried. I picked him up and sank to the floor with my back against the wall, and we cried together. I still remember his eyes looking into mine as he squinted and wailed, his body squirming in obvious distress. I felt like such a failure, inadequate and useless.

In that moment, I knew I had to do *something*. We couldn't go on like this. I certainly couldn't expect my infant son to change. I was the grown-up. It was up to me.

Despite feeling that I knew nothing at all about babies, one thing I did know a lot about was sound—particularly patterns in sound. I walked into the kitchen and pulled out an old notebook. The first step, it seemed to me, was simply to describe the sound of the cries. Perhaps if I wrote down the sounds and patterns, I could remember the different cries and what worked with solving them.

I named each cry based on the phonetic sound that I could hear within it. This cry had "e" in it; that cry had more of an "n" sound; this other cry had an "aw" sound.

It was a start. I continued to keep a "cry diary," and when Tom cried—which was often!—I wrote down the phonetic name of the sound, and if I did something that calmed the crying, I wrote that down, too. I created a chart with the name of the cry and the matching solution. I started to see which sounds consistently matched which solutions. Slowly, things started to become smoother.

More and more, Tom and I were in sync. I was even able to take him out to a local mall—an outing that would have been impossible before I had started charting his cries. As we walked around the shops, I saw other parents there with their babies. And I realized that *those babies were making the same cries that Tom did!*

In those cries, I detected the phonetic sound signatures that eventually became the Dunstan Baby Language. I also noticed that when a parent responded with one of my identified solutions for a specific cry, the baby would stop crying. If not, the baby would continue crying. That, too, was a revelation: I had assumed that each baby had different cries and that my understanding Tom's cries was just a mother's intuition finally kicking in. In fact, I'd felt incredibly inadequate that it had taken so long for me to figure out what my son was telling me. Now I realized I wasn't alone.

I started talking with other parents, asking about their experiences with their babies' cries. Some asked how I had learned to decode my baby's cries. I told them about my chart. Many wanted a copy, so I shared my chart and asked them to let me know how things went. Within a day of giving out the chart for the first time, I got responses from all the parents I had given it to! They had, in turn, given it to their friends and shared it in their baby groups. They were telling stories of how this little chart had transformed their lives! It was very humbling.

Eventually the chart was forwarded to a few doctors, who called me wanting to know how I'd created it and how the sounds worked. They wanted to be able to give new parents something to help guide them in the first weeks and months with their babies. I realized I had stumbled onto an insight that could help families and, I hoped, prevent anyone from feeling the way I had that night when Tom and I had cried together.

the search for scientific verification

I COME FROM AN ACADEMIC FAMILY in which proof and data are important. While I knew this "language" worked, I had no idea why. My father, who was a doctor of child psychology and a specialist in educational testing, suggested I gather samples of the cries and document the solutions. Then together we could develop and start a real research project.

I began by advertising in the local paper for mothers who would be willing to participate in an observational video. I got many responses. I went to their homes and filmed their babies crying and the mothers' attempts to pacify their babies. I put it all into the computer and then just sat and listened, editing the footage into the different cries the babies made. It was so exciting to hear in all these infants' cries the very same sounds that Tom had made!

Next I had to prove that a particular sound related consistently to a particular need. Using processes called interventions and a "control" type situation, I was able to test whether a given word corresponded with a given need. I had to make sure that the crying didn't stop simply because the infant was picked up, for example, but rather because that particular need was met. I made a video with three of the "words" I was sure of. (I eventually called these the "newborn words.")

Then I advertised again, seeking mothers who wanted to try a new approach to caring for their baby. I was deluged with replies! Again, I filmed the mothers with their babies. Then I interviewed them about how they interpreted and resolved their babies' needs. I left them with the newborn words video and a description of what to do when they heard the newborn words within their baby's cries. Ten days later, I filmed and interviewed them again.

The results were amazing. Not only could all the parents hear the sounds within their baby's cries, but many were able to associate the sound with a need. The impact on many of the parents was dramatic. One couple's relationship was in serious jeopardy because of their baby's constant crying and need for attention. They were in continual conflict over how the baby should be managed. Based on what they learned from my tape, together they were able to calm their baby completely, resolve their conflict over the baby, and heal their relationship. What a profound effect this "language" could have on other people!

The other remarkable result was the improvement in the parents' self-esteem. In just the ten days they'd been using the system, there had been a distinct change in how they felt about themselves as parents and in the atmosphere at home.

I remember the day I realized we might be onto something really profound for parents and babies. I was visiting a friend and her husband to help with their crying baby. As soon as my friend opened the door, I could feel the tension in the house. My friend was a highly organized, competent professional who had always run a very orderly home.

But now things were different. The house was a mess. My friend looked as if she was about to burst into tears. Her husband was banging things in the kitchen in the way that lets you know a couple was having an argument when the doorbell rang.

Two weeks later, I returned to see how they were doing with the classification system. The house was neat. My friend was smiling. The baby was playing happily nearby. Not only did they offer me a cup of tea (an automatic Aussie courtesy), but they actually were organized enough to serve me one!

I've seen that dramatic change—in parents, baby, and home environment—replicated over and over since then.

Independent research conducted with mothers in Australia, the United States, and the United Kingdom in 2006 and 2007 showed just what a positive impact knowing the system has on the families of newborns.

- 90 percent of all mothers, regardless of how many previous children they had, found value in knowing the Dunstan Baby Language.
- 100 percent of first-time mothers reported the system to be an invaluable tool enabling them to meet their baby's needs.
- 70 percent of parents said their baby settled faster.
- 50 percent experienced better feeding results.
- 50 percent reported longer and better quality sleep for both them and their baby.
- 70 percent of parents reported feeling more confident, relaxed, and in control.
- 50 percent of mothers felt they were more bonded with their baby.
- Two out of three fathers reported that the reduced levels of stress resulted in a better feeling at home between themselves and their wives.

Since those first days and months of working out the Dunstan Baby Language, I've worked with professionals in linguistics, sociology, pediatrics, and psychology. I've appeared on national TV, traveled the world, and worked with families from royal princesses to the very poor—all of whom in the end are simply parents yearning to understand their baby's cries.

Listening to hundreds of babies, I've discovered the same complexity in infant's voices that I hear in adults'. A baby who has been up screaming two nights earlier will have "holes" in his vocalizations, just like adults who've been under significant stress. A baby who is having a difficult time emotionally or who is struggling with frequently being overwhelmed will have a quicker pulse in her voice than one more at peace with her surroundings. I'm awed and humbled to think that this system has helped so many parents create a calmer, more comfortable home environment for these wondrous little beings.

how to use this book

YOU MAY FEEL you want to jump ahead and learn all the words at once! But try not to. The system isn't complicated, but as with learning any new skill (especially a new language), if you go too fast at first, it's easy to get confused or overwhelmed. (And if you're a new parent, you're already probably on a steep learning curve!)

So go slowly. I recommend you follow the book's instructions in order and make sure that you can hear a given word within the baby's cry before moving on. The words are grouped and related by how they sound and when you would hear them. Practice saying each sound yourself, and watch yourself in a mirror. Feeling your own body and voice produce the words will help you see and hear when your baby is producing them. If you have trouble, log on to the Calm the Crying website (calmthecrying.com), and check out the sound and video samples.

Following each group of words is a section outlining calming solutions to try, from special ways to hold your baby to diapering and feeding techniques and tips. While this book doesn't cover all aspects of baby care, I try to provide a broad array of solutions for calming your baby's crying. The solutions are relevant not only for the words but also more generally for the development stage your baby will be in when you hear that sound (newborn, about six weeks, and about twelve weeks). Even if your baby is older than twelve weeks, this book can help you, as he will continue to use some of the words, and the timetable for when the words emerge (and eventually disappear) varies.

Finally, have fun! This book is meant to take the pressure off and help you as well as your baby. If you feel stressed while trying to understand your baby's cries, stop, breathe, and do what you would normally do when listening carefully to what someone is saying. With practice, you'll soon be able to hear and identify your baby's cries with ease.

A SPECIAL CAUTION

If at any time you feel that you have reached your limit, or if you find yourself raising your voice to your baby, or being more physical or rough with your baby, these may be signs that you've reached your limit and need to find a safe alternative. Place the baby in a safe area, such as his crib, and leave the room. Call a friend or relative to help. This is the one situation in which it is better to shut the door and leave the baby to cry. Once you are feeling more in control, attend to your baby and seek help. Discuss some solutions with your doctor, as you may be suffering from postpartum depression or another issue that would be helped by consulting a qualified professional.

ACKNOWLEDGMENTS

THANK YOU to the many parents who have been such a source of inspiration. From the first moms who trialed the system to the many others who continue to help either through their support or continuing research.

Thank you to Tom Dunstan. Your first cry has made millions of other babies' lives easier. Your voice has allowed others to be heard, and I'm sure that when you grow up, whatever you become will have the same qualities. Thank you for being you, and for being the kind, thoughtful, and intelligent person you are.

Thank you to Kasey Byrne, my right-hand man, with the unique ability to translate Priscillaese into easy-to-understand concepts, both written and verbal. You are truly an amazing person and an exceptional friend, and I am so blessed to have you in my life.

Thank you to Megan Newman, who oozes intelligence, kindness, and professionalism, and wraps that up in a way to support her writers to do their best possible work. Your light touch but strength in conviction is a breath of fresh air, and I am a very lucky person to have you as my publisher.

Thank you to Toni Sciarra Poyner, who managed to make the process of editing painless and uplifting. You added clarification to difficult areas, improving the balance between information and empathy, and you did it all with grace, integrity, curiosity, and humor.

Thank you to Philip Beazley, who has answered my many, many questions patiently and not only supported me to be able to move forward, but also provided the safety to do so. You are a very remarkable soul.

Thank you to Bob Stein for your insights and legal support, especially in your interest in the finished product and not just the contract.

I have been very fortunate to have had a collection of amazing, wise, and supportive people who have influenced me in many different ways. Thank you especially to: Adil Edgu, Mark Tognolini, Alexandra Van Rijn, Lorna Elliot, Prue Ives, Terese Mudgway, Lisa Higgins, Jill Miller, Oprah Winfrey, Rupert Murdoch, Michelle Conn, Natalie White, Jessica Thomas, David Wilson, Kelli Harris, Dee Barry Lester, Linda Lagasse, Nadine Watt, Mark Rivett, and, of course, my father, Max Dunstan.

the how and why of your baby's cries

As with most challenges, understanding how and why something happens is the first step toward solving the problem.

a universal language based on reflex

EACH WORD I'VE IDENTIFIED in the Dunstan Baby Language is based on a natural reflex action caused by your baby's physical needs.

Here's how it works: First the baby's body produces the reflex; then he adds sound, in the form of a cry. This combination of reflex and sound creates a unique "sound signature" specific to that need. I call this sound signature a "word." This word, once understood, will tell us the need associated with the reflex.

For example, when a baby is hungry, she will start to suck. As she begins to cry, adding sound to the sucking reflex, the word for "hunger" is produced.

It's important to remember that these communications aren't conscious the way those of adults are. The baby doesn't realize she's hungry and decide to make the sound signature for hunger. A baby's hungry body makes a reflex (sucking), wedded to vocal sound, which we can interpret once we're sensitized to hear it within the baby's cry.

Our ancestors may have had innate knowledge of babies' cries, passed down from mother to daughter. Some of you may be lucky enough to know a wise older person who can hear a baby cry and know exactly what to do. Some combination of experience, intuition, and an attentive ear helps her understand the baby's needs. These days, many of us have babies later in life and often live far away from our mothers. Many new parents weren't brought up in a world of younger siblings and extended family—many a new mother has told me that the first diaper she ever changed was her newborn's. Depending on our culture and our family circumstances, caring for babies can be largely an isolated experience. We need the wisdom of our baby's cries given to us in a modern form, so we have a chance to understand our baby's primal language.

A PRIMAL-REFLEX PRIMER

When your baby is first born, your doctor will check your newborn's health, including making sure that certain reflexes are working properly. The presence and strength of primal reflexes are used to evaluate your baby's neurological function and development. Primitive reflexes happen automatically, without conscious thought, and without the involvement of the conscious part of the brain. Often a friendly doctor will check these with you observing, so you can see how they work, and what amazing things your newborn baby is innately programmed to do.

The most common reflexes tested are:

- *The sucking reflex.* When you put your finger to your baby's lips, she will instinctively start to suck vigorously.

- *The rooting reflex.* When you touch his cheek or the side of his mouth, your baby will turn his head as if searching for a nipple.

- *The palmar grasp.* When your baby's hand tightens around your finger.

- *The tonic neck reflex.* When your baby's head is turned to one side, the arm the baby faces will be stretched out and the other arm will be bent upward at the elbow.

- *The Babinski reflex.* When you stroke the soles of your baby's feet, her toes fan outward.

- *The plantar reflex.* When the foot sole is stroked, your baby's foot and toes curl inward.

- *The placing reflex.* When you touch the sole of your baby's foot, he extends his leg.

- *The stepping reflex.* When held upright, your baby takes walking steps if his feet were placed on a flat surface.

- *The Moro (or startle) reflex.* Often triggered by loud sounds and sudden movements, in this reflex your baby extends her arms wide and high, then bends them back in toward the body.

Most infantile primitive reflexes do not last beyond the first year, and many have been repressed by six months of age. Usually the baby no longer needs the function provided by the reflex, the baby integrates the reflex into developing movements and behaviors, or the baby simply outgrows the reflex.

Not all reflexes are meant to disappear (adults have reflexes we use daily, such as the blinking reflex, the cough reflex, and the yawn reflex; there are also the sneeze reflex and the gag reflex). Doctors also check adults' reflexes to gain insight into our health (such as tapping your knee with a small rubber hammer to test the knee-jerk reflex).

crying: a normal, necessary reflex?

AS SOON AS your baby is born, he will cry as he takes his first breath. Your doctor will check for that first cry and, if it doesn't happen, will encourage it. From that point on, crying is automatically your baby's main form of communication. My many years of studying vocalization have led me to believe that a baby's cry is itself a reflex action.

Think about the reflexive sounds adults make. When something suddenly scares us, we cry out. When someone tickles us, most of us laugh. Every sneeze, cough, or hiccup has an identifying sound that we recognize instantly, even without seeing the action. Other primal sounds we also recognize: the sound of a couple making love in the hotel room next to ours is unmistakable. There are clear differences in the sounds we make when in pain, depending on the type of pain. A sharp, quick pain elicits a sharp yelp; an aching, constant hurt brings forth a longer groan.

These are all sounds synonymous with an action happening in our bodies, and these sounds are universal to our species, understandable in any language. Even if it's hard to view an infant's crying as a reflex, clearly our bodies make many universal, understandable, reflexive sounds. The sounds within your baby's cry are the ones I want to help you understand.

the cry-respond-bond cycle

A NEWBORN INFANT'S CRY is a powerful motivator for parents and other adults, activating a primal anxiety that prompts parents to respond. We are preprogrammed on an elemental level to hear and react to a baby's cry. Even adults who aren't related to the infant or responsible for her care will have a reaction to the cry. How many times have you been sitting in a café, oblivious to traffic sounds or even sirens—but unavoidably distracted when a baby starts to cry? An infant's cry actually creates a physical discomfort in us, incenting us to do what is necessary to make it stop.

In fact, there is an ideal caregiving pattern, common across many cultures and geographies, for attending to the primal needs of an infant. For the parents, it means Mom and Dad understanding why their baby is crying, addressing the baby's needs, being able to settle the baby, and feeling like good parents. For the baby, it means feeling secure that her cries are understood and that her needs are consistently met. When the baby's needs are met, the baby cries less. Less crying means more time for baby and parents to bond, building the baby's self-esteem, enhancing parents' confidence, and forging stronger family units.

We now understand that bonding and attachment are essential for a child to grow up to be a functional member of society. Responsive caregiving directly influences how children relate to the world and to others for the rest of their lives—and it may even affect intelligence: a study, "The Relationship Between Quality of Attachment in Infancy and IQ in Kindergarten" conducted at University of Leiden, the Netherlands, showed that babies in the securely attached group attained higher IQ readings, with results showing as early as kindergarten.

Parents who are well bonded with their child do better, too: they have a higher tolerance for normal parenting challenges such as crying, sleep deprivation, and the lifestyle changes parenting requires.

We parents know this in practical terms: it's very hard to bond with a crying baby—even harder when you doubt your ability to help the crying child. A continually crying baby requires the caregiver to function in a very high-stress situation: the baby has acute physical needs, and the main goal is to stop the crying and try to manage the situation. This is not a time for staring lovingly into each other's eyes!

Babies who cry a lot also often become exhausted, limiting the time available for positive, loving interaction. Parent and child get locked into a problem-reaction cycle, with little opportunity to get to know each other in peace, without distress.

Parents, too, can become overwhelmed by a baby's continual crying, which can increase feelings of helplessness and possibly the risk of postpartum depression. A study conducted in several European countries by the Norwegian University of Science and Technology showed that "both infantile colic and prolonged crying were associated with high maternal depression scores. Most noteworthy, infantile colic at two months of age was associated with high maternal depression scores four months later."

Symptoms of postpartum depression include lack of interest in the baby, negative feelings toward the baby, feelings of worthlessness and guilt, and in extreme cases, severe effects such as suicide and hurting one's baby. Shaken baby syndrome is correlated with parental stress, often due to an inconsolable, crying baby and a parent without the tools to cope. As I've said, continual crying is a high-stress situation. It's hard enough to try to address the cause of a baby's crying, much less to have the objectivity to recognize our own stress level or take precautions against a dangerous reaction.

Babies can stress relationships, too. An eight-year study from the University of Denver showed that in 90 percent of couples, marital bliss declined within a year after the birth of their first child. Divorce statistics show that one in eight couples with "problem babies" will end their relationship within eighteen months. In my research, I have found that how supported a mother feels by her partner will be remembered for many years to come, and feeling insufficiently supported is often the catalyst for a declining relationship. This is especially true for parents of babies who are very vocal—and it's a direct result, I believe, of the isolation of and lack of information and support for new parents.

The beginning of any relationship can set the tone for its future. Parents who feel inadequate or unable to meet their newborn's needs can carry this feeling of disconnection throughout their parenting lives. During my research for "Sensory Studies of Elementary School Children," which formed the basis of my book *Child Sense*, I met many parents who said they could never understand their children, even when they were babies. It was heartbreaking to hear a mother say, "My child and I never really got on, even from birth—she never seemed to like me." A parent who feels unable to understand or meet her baby's needs may withdraw emotionally from the infant, which can be hard to rectify.

Understanding your baby's needs through her cries is often the critical missing piece of the parenting puzzle that we have forgotten, or never learned, and will set us on the course to becoming joyful, confident experts in our baby's care.

tips for learning your baby's language

UNDERSTANDING DAWNS
My wife had just had our third child. I had left the hospital for a meeting with a possible new client who was releasing a DVD on

infant cries. Yes, it was Priscilla! As I left the maternity ward, hearing all the babies' cries, I remember feeling skeptical. In the meeting, I watched the DVD, and I must admit it was pretty cute watching all those babies saying the same thing. However, it didn't really hit me until I went back to the maternity ward after work. I walked up the same corridor I'd walked down a few hours earlier—and whereas before I could only hear babies crying, now I was hearing neh, eh, and owh. It was amazing! It was as if someone had given me new ears, and I could understand what these babies were saying! —STEVE

In my work with parents, the moment I love best is seeing the proverbial light go on as they hear the sounds. They almost always exclaim, "My baby says that!" or "I've heard that sound before!" The realization that their baby has actually been speaking to them is a life-altering one. Once you know what to listen for, you'll be able to associate infant sounds with your baby's needs as easily as you recognize a sneeze or a cough.

WHAT TO LISTEN FOR

Each infant cry has been translated into a phonetic word for easy identification. I also provide a few English words that sound similar to or rhyme with the sound your baby will make, to help you know what to listen for.

WHAT TO OBSERVE

Most of us don't spend much time thinking about how we produce sound, but between my training as a singer, violinist, and baby listener, I've studied it a lot. The structures inside our mouth, and indeed our entire face, throat, and lungs, are exquisitely designed and able to work in concert, with great subtlety, to create thousands of sound combinations and variations. If we think of ourselves as an instrument, we are one of the most marvelous.

Our entire body is involved in sound: when we move, sit, lie down, or straighten up, we loosen or tighten different muscles, which produces a different tone—because we have changed the instrument. In the same way that one finger placed on a violin string changes its pitch, so the precise placement of our tongue in our mouth changes the sounds we make.

Your baby has amazing vocal abilities, though he's still learning to control and coordinate them. In the chapters that follow, you'll learn how to observe your baby's mouth, tongue, and sound production as part of understanding his cries.

FOCUS ON THE PRE-CRY

You know those first few noises your baby makes, before he really starts crying? They're what is called the pre-cry. The pre-cry is incredibly important. The phonetic words are clearest—complete and isolated—in the pre-cry. That's the ideal time to decode and respond to your baby's words: when he's communicating a need and isn't yet frustrated, anxious, and screaming.

Because your baby's words are reflexive extensions of processes in his body, they're not something he controls. Nor can he control how clearly he enunciates these sounds. You have to be listening carefully.

So when your baby begins to make sounds, before he starts to cry, tune in and listen to the phonetic sounds. Look at what his body and mouth are doing. Once your baby starts screaming, the sounds are still there, but they're distorted, mixed with other sounds, and harder to distinguish. It's harder to soothe him then, too. In that way, babies aren't that different from adults: once we're angry and raise our voices, it's harder for others to understand us and calm us down.

The Dunstan Baby Language acts as an early warning system, helping parents to recognize a need before the baby becomes truly upset, and to more quickly calm the crying.

TRY MAKING THE SOUND YOURSELF

Try describing to someone what the itch of a mosquito bite feels like. Hard, isn't it? But if they've had that kind of itch themselves, they'll understand. We learn best through our own experiences—and when those experiences are rooted in our bodies, or *kinesthetic*, they're incredibly vivid and memorable.

That's why I want you to actually try to make the sound signatures, not just read my descriptions. It lets you feel what your baby's body is doing and hear an approximation of the sound your baby will make. It won't be exact, as the variables of age, teeth, and conscious thought come into play, but it will help anchor the sound signature in your memory.

For example, suppose you notice that your baby is bringing her tongue up to the roof of her mouth and then moving it down, repetitively. If you try mimicking this action, you'll instantly feel that you want to swallow, and you'll realize that your tongue is making a sucking motion. This will help you to remember that the sucking reflex is attached to the hunger cry and enable you to hear the "neh" sound your baby makes when she needs to be fed.

Looking at yourself in the mirror as you make the sound will give you visual cues to watch for with your crying baby.

LISTEN FOR THE WORD WITHIN YOUR BABY'S CRY

Even if your baby is well past the pre-cry, you can still hear the word signaling her need if you can filter out the other sounds she's making and focus on one word.

If you've ever learned a foreign language or traveled to a place where you don't speak the language, you know that you become adept at listening for the few words you know and picking them out of the cacophony around you. Perhaps you know the word for "thank you." You may hear and understand it without comprehending any of the words before and after it.

It's similar when listening for words in your baby's cries. You'll recognize the words you know, even if you're confused by all the other sounds you're hearing. Your baby helps, too: his body and reflexes are very adamant, so when he needs to be fed, he will make that reflexive sound over and over until he is fed.

you hear the word! now what?

I'VE ORGANIZED THIS BOOK to help you quickly access the information you need to identify and meet your baby's needs. Once you hear the word, simply turn to the chapter covering solutions for that word. You can try them all, or pick the one that works best.

ADDITIONAL TIPS

- *Try breaking the scream cycle.* Often, just picking up a screaming baby is enough to calm her a bit and give her a chance to "speak more clearly." Then listen closely during this short reprieve.

- *Remember, she'll repeat.* The baby will repeat her need and the reflex sound as long as she has the need—or until a more urgent need supersedes it. If you don't understand at first, you'll have more opportunities!

- *Get it on tape.* Sometimes recording your baby using your smartphone or video camera and playing it back afterward can help you identify her cries in a calmer setting.

- *Get help.* If after reading this book and practicing, you're still have difficulty identifying sounds, log on to the Calm the Crying website (calmthecrying.com) and click on the sounds to hear babies saying them. You can also view instructional videos to help you gain a better understanding.

- *When in doubt, pick up your baby.* The aim is to calm and soothe your baby at all times. Even if you don't understand your baby's cries, it's better that she feel you're there rather than that she's been left alone. However, if you're having difficulty controlling your reactions to the crying, are raising your voice to the baby, or are being rougher with the baby, you may be reaching your limit. In that case, put the baby in a safe place such as her crib, leave the room, call a friend or relative for help, and consult your doctor as well.

newborn words

□

Newborn words are three words that your baby will be saying from the moment he is born. They are the words for hunger ("neh"), tiredness ("owh"), and burping ("eh"). They are the three most useful and important words for everyday care. Understanding these three words will help you to address the top three concerns for a newborn baby. Once you've mastered these words, you can proceed to the next set, moving either at your own pace or in line with the age of your baby. While these three words are newborn words, your baby will keep saying them after the six-week mark, and you may find yourself referring to this section and these words even with an older baby.

CHAPTER 1
"neh": "i'm hungry"

W HEN YOUR BABY BECOMES HUNGRY, he'll start to fuss, and you'll hear the sound "neh" within his cry.

The word "neh" is a vocalization based on the sucking reflex the infant makes when first becoming hungry.

The sucking reflex is known as a primitive reflex. It is present in all healthy, full-term babies, and in all but the smallest of preterm babies. This reflex actually starts before birth, while the infant is still in the womb, and it's one of the most important primitive reflexes, as without it the baby cannot feed.

The best way to recognize if your baby is saying "neh" is to look in his mouth. If he's making sucking motions with his tongue and he's started to cry, you will hear the "neh" sound.

Typically, a baby will start to make sucking motions just as he's starting to get hungry, before the more aggressive crying and rooting around that denote a truly hungry baby. The benefit of listening for "neh" is that you'll hear it and can respond before the baby gets distressed and upset—which is helpful, as all parents know that babies can get very hungry, very fast.

A baby's stomach is small, and his diet consists of easy-to-digest proteins such as whey and casein, so he becomes hungry after a short time. A few hours after your baby has last eaten, his glucose levels will drop, causing his little body to chemically and physically react.

A baby can be happy, playing, and appreciating the world one minute, and begin screaming with desperate hunger the next.

what "neh" sounds like

IN ORDER TO UNDERSTAND "neh" more fully, try to replicate it yourself.

Place your tongue behind your top teeth and push it up to the roof of your mouth. Now, try adding sound. You'll notice that the only sound you can make comes through your nose and sounds like "nnnnnn."

As you make the "nnnnnn" sound, open your mouth a little and start moving your tongue in a sucking motion. As your tongue moves away from the top of your mouth, you will notice the "nnn" changes to a sound like "eih." Put the sounds together, and you have "neh."

You can hear "neh" at the beginning of English words like "neck," "nest," "net," and "never." Notice when you say these words that your tongue starts up high behind your teeth at the roof of your mouth and moves downward. This is the tongue motion that is the same for the word "neh."

how "neh" is made

WHEN ADULTS GET HUNGRY, we feel hunger pangs, our saliva increases, and we can become agitated with the need to eat. When newborn babies become hungry, their saliva increases, too—but while an adult might be able to swallow, the baby, often lying down or held horizontally, needs to suck to clear her mouth.

So, with this onset of hunger, your baby will start the preliminary motions of sucking, and in her discomfort she'll start to cry.

The actual formation of "neh" is based on both the baby's sucking reflex and the motion of the baby's tongue against the roof of her mouth, manipulating the sound of her cry.

When you're learning to hear "neh," looking for visual cues can help. When your baby is saying "neh," you may notice that his mouth is half open and his tongue moves forward in a sucking motion. Once the baby is fully engaged in the sucking reflex, his tongue moves in rhythmic cycles of extension and retraction, with little or no lateral movement. As it extends, it flattens along the top of his mouth, stopping and descending before it gets to the lips. You will be able to observe the flattening and slight cupping of the tongue if there is a nipple or finger in the baby's mouth; his tongue will flatten against it, and suction will happen on the retraction. It is on the extension that the sound "neh" occurs, being produced in an empty mouth, as the baby's body prepares for food.

Your baby's lips will move also, and he will be rooting around trying to suck something—his hand, your finger—all in the primal hope that it is a nipple.

hearing "neh"

"NEH" WILL BEGIN in a quiet, distinct way, within the pre-cry stage, moving to the crying stage as the discomfort of hunger increases her crying. The frequency of the sound "neh" will increase, but so too will the other sounds around it, resulting in more "noise" being heard around the word "neh." Because this is not a conscious language but rather a primal sound happening almost by accident, the more distressed or upset your baby becomes, the more "noise" is heard around "neh."

You can use the analogy of a sentence. Generally a sentence has one or two key words surrounded by less important ones. For example, you can simply say "hungry," or use it in a short sentence: "I am hungry," or in a longer sentence: "I am getting very hungry now!" If we swap the word "neh" for "hungry" and translate those sentences into cries, we hear a simple "neh" ("hungry") during the pre-cry or fussing stage, "eghjy neh vhhlj" ("I am hungry") during the normal crying stage, and "hjfkjhj neh hjhdjfh neh neh jkjkku" ("I am getting very hungry now!") during the desperate crying stage.

You may hear something in the cry similar to a stutter, in which the more upset a person is, the harder it is to get the word out and be understood. Your baby will keep saying "neh" until she has been fed, but of course you'd like to meet her needs quickly and head off those desperate cries. Keep your baby close to you or within easy earshot, so you will be able to more easily hear her words.

CHAPTER 2
"owh": "i'm tired"

WHEN YOU HEAR your baby saying "owh," it means that his body is becoming tired, he's getting sleepy, and he's ready for bed. He is yawning, and that reflexive yawn is producing an "owh" sound within his cry. You will hear "owh" within his pre-cry sounds and also within his full-cry vocalization.

You'll likely hear this sound before seeing the more traditional signs of tiredness, such as jerky movements, eye rubbing, and agitated fist-to-mouth movements.

It's good to be able to spot the early signs of sleepiness, since babies, like adults, have an easier time falling asleep soon after they start to feel sleepy rather than later, when they might get a second wind or might become overtired—which, paradoxically, can make it harder to go to sleep.

Babies, especially young ones, are extremely susceptible to becoming overtired. In fact, once a baby is at the eye-rubbing or jerky-movements stage, she is past being comfortably tired and is going to need extra attention to fall asleep. You'll start hearing "owh" in the "comfortably tired" stage, and you'll know it's time to put her down to sleep.

what "owh" sounds like

YOU CAN HEAR PHONETIC SOUNDS similar to "owh" at the end of English words like "cow," "now," "wow," "plow," and of course in the sound we make when we hurt ourselves—"ow!" Say that word right now, and you'll notice that your tongue stays at the bottom of your mouth, and that the closing of your lips and throat changes the sound from "o" to "ow."

You can make the "owh" sound simply by yawning and adding sound as you exhale. Open your mouth wide and push your tongue flat against your bottom teeth. Inhale, opening the back of your throat, and start to yawn. As you exhale, allow the sound of your voice to flow naturally. You'll hear an elongated "ou." Continue making the sound as you close your mouth, and it changes from "ou" to a "wh." It is the combination of the "ou" and the "wh" that makes the "owh" sound.

how "owh" is made

AS YOU'VE JUST DISCOVERED, a yawn is an inhalation in which the palate and jaw muscles stretch to form an oval shape. The mouth opens, the jaw drops, and the tongue slides back and flattens, producing a narrow opening between the tongue and the back of your throat (the pharyngeal wall). This lowers the larynx, or voice box, which, along with the closing of the mouth on the exhalation, produces the vowel part of the "owh" sound. The finishing "wh" occurs as the cheeks widen while air is still being expelled.

34

Take a closer look at your baby's mouth as she says "owh," and you'll clearly see the oval shape of her mouth, followed by the pulling back and lowering of her tongue, which makes the cavity of her mouth larger and more open. These movements, combined with the expansion and contraction of her diaphragm as she yawns, create the "owh" sound. You may see her eyes squinting as she makes the sound.

Researchers are not yet completely clear on why humans and other animals yawn, though they do know that it's a sign of fatigue and probably also a general sign of a change in alertness. Interestingly, it has also been shown that while the "contagious yawn" happens among adult humans, it doesn't happen with infants. It seems that when an infant yawns, it is purely for his own physical need.

hearing "owh"

WHILE BABIES YAWN much more often than adults, a baby's yawn is not necessarily as obvious as an adult's, so "owh" can be a very soft sound, easily missed in a noisy household or public space.

If his "owh" is not heard, your baby will start to whine, with those sounds mixed in and around the "owh." Then he'll start to cry, adding those sounds, too.

As with the other sounds, "owh" becomes harder to hear once your infant is screaming, so you want to try to catch the sound before it becomes part of a cry. That's also your best window for being able to settle your baby down to sleep with less fuss. When you respond to the baby's natural desire to sleep, you may avoid the hours of rocking, patting, and pacing typically associated with putting babies to sleep.

CHAPTER 3

"eh": "i need to burp"

T HE SOUND YOUR BABY MAKES when he has wind is "eh." It comes from the burping reflex.

"Eh" means that your baby has air trapped in his upper digestive system and the muscles there are automatically contracting to squeeze out the air. "Eh" is the resulting sound.

what "eh" sounds like

THE SOUND OF A BURP is universally recognized, but the sound adults make when we burp is different from the sound your baby makes as he tries to burp. "Eh" is not the sound of an actual burp, but the sound of your baby *trying to* burp.

So, what's happening when our body tries to burp? Gas is building up and becoming uncomfortable. The chest muscles are contracting in an attempt to push the air out. Our chest may feel tight and we may experience a sensation almost like indigestion. Our adult body knows instinctively how to react to that feeling of pressure. We may move, stand up, lean forward, hold our breath, or drink from a glass of water to help our body push out the air.

If we're trying to suppress the burp, we may be visibly uncomfortable, but even then we can usually adjust ourselves somewhat in order to move the air bubble out.

When your baby is saying "eh," she's feeling the sensation you feel just before a burp, when your body is struggling to expel the air.

But what if your body was positioned incorrectly, so you couldn't release the air? And what if you couldn't move, sit up, or lean in a way that would help? That's how your baby feels.

Babies, especially newborns, need us to help them burp. They let us know by saying "eh, eh, eh," and by wriggling around, trying to help themselves.

how "eh" is made

THE SIGNIFICANT PART of "eh" is the short, restricted "e" at the beginning of the sound. Phonetically it sounds similar to the "e" sound in words like "escalate," "escape," "extra," and "every."

To make "eh," fill your upper chest with air, close your throat muscles, and try to push the air out with your chest muscles. Now release your throat muscles for just a second to let some air escape. You'll make the "eh" sound. Notice it is short and sharp, with a distinct start to the "e" and a strong, breathy "h."

It can help to understand what is going on in your baby's body, as burping is quite a complex set of coordinated physical activities. The diaphragm descends to increase abdominal pressure and decrease pressure in the chest, allowing air from the stomach to move to the esophagus. The lower esophageal sphincter or muscle must be open, so that the escaping air can pass from the stomach into the esophagus. The upper esophageal sphincter also needs to be relaxed, so that air can pass more easily from the esophagus into the throat, and the larynx must be closed to protect the lungs from any liquid that may come up the esophagus along with the air from the stomach.

This process is made all the harder by the baby's inability to move, sit up, or otherwise get vertical to help release the gas. Newborns also have immature digestive systems that they've only just started to use. The baby is learning to feed as well, and often he will suck in air as he feeds, sucks his fists, sucks his pacifier, or cries, or simply because his body is learning to work in a more coordinated way.

But air intake is also more usual than you may think. As adults we still take in air; but we find it easy and automatic to release it. We actually burp throughout the day—especially if we drink carbonated beverages, eat certain foods that make us gassy, or are at that age and stage when burping impresses our friends. We have control and the ability to adjust our bodies to remove the air when needed, but a baby has to rely on others to help him.

hearing "eh"

WHEN YOUR BABY'S BODY is trying to release trapped air in the form of a burp, you will hear "eh, eh, eh" in the pre-cry stage. As your baby's discomfort increases, the sound will elongate into an "eeeehhhhh." You will also notice that the sides of the baby's mouth are turned up a bit and that the mouth is only slightly open.

It's time to help your baby by picking her up and following the burping methods in chapter 6. The shorter the "eh," the easier it is to address. If it's a clear "eh, eh, eh," simply pick up your baby, give her a quick little tap on her back, and *presto*! Problem solved.

The more elongated the sound, as in "eeeehhhh," the more assisting you'll need to do to help her release the gas. You may use more burping holds and some of the more involved burping methods.

The timing of the sound will also help you to determine the type of burping technique needed. If "eh" happens right after a feeding, you don't want the baby to spit up along with the burp. In this case, you would opt for a slower burping method in a more upright position. If "eh" happens more than an hour after a feeding, an over-the-shoulder hold with a repeated up-and-down backrub will probably work best.

How can you tell when your baby is done burping and there isn't another air bubble or burp waiting? Your baby will burp and stop saying "eh." Sometimes you won't hear a loud burp, but you'll feel your baby's body relax, indicating the buildup of gas inside your baby's stomach has dispersed.

CHAPTER 4

"neh" solutions

NO MORE RUSHING AT FEEDING TIME

The hunger word is the one I've really picked up on. I used to think that Emmy got hungry very quickly, and I was always so stressed at having to rush to feed her. Now that I know that her sounds are actually telling me something, I try to keep her close by and listen for that distinct "n" sound. I've found that she generally starts with a quiet "neh, neh" while she's still observing the world. This is my cue that she will be hungry soon, so I can start to get prepared. By the time she's starting to say "neh" more frequently or is beginning to cry, I'm ready to feed her. –JUSTINE

"Neh" is the word you will hear in your baby's cries when she's hungry. It is made by adding sound to the sucking reflex. Hearing this word in your baby's pre-cry allows you some time to prepare for feeding. Below we'll discuss solutions for breast-feeding, supplementation, and bottle-feeding.

feeding routine: be guided by your baby

PUSHING YOUR BABY into a feeding routine at this young age will end in tears for all. If a routine is needed, better to approach it from the baby's point of view and form a baby-guided schedule, which involves making a schedule around your baby's natural inclinations and guiding her toward the pattern you need to make life at home functional. I discuss baby-guided schedules in the opener to part 3.

feeding methods: a flexible, baby-centered approach

WHEN PEOPLE TALK about feeding babies, much of the discussion revolves around the delivery method—that is, whether you're breast-feeding or bottle-feeding your baby.

The Dunstan Baby Language is baby centered, so when I work with parents, we look at feeding from the baby's perspective: focusing not on the delivery system but on what the baby is getting and what the baby's cry tells us about that.

If a breast-fed baby is frequently crying "eairh," the word for having gas (see part 2), we'll look at his mother's diet to see if she's taking in foods that her baby is sensitive to, among other possible causes. If a formula-fed baby is crying "heir" frequently, indicating skin or other surface discomfort (which we'll also explore in part 2), we'll investigate whether he might have an allergy issue with the formula.

Babies can be fed breast milk, formula, or both (known as supplement feeding). While some babies receive breast milk or formula exclusively, I often find that babies start with only breast milk, then get breast milk and formula (with breast milk fed from the breast and/or bottle), and finally receive only formula. We'll talk about these phases in more detail below, and what each means to both parents and baby.

the three phases of feeding

AS MENTIONED, from my experience working with and researching parents and feeding, I have concluded that there are three phases that many families go through when feeding an infant. They usually start with breast-feeding, then move into supplementation, and finally into bottle-feeding formula (perhaps also offering it in a sippy cup or by spoon). The length of these phases is different for every parent and baby. Some mothers breast-feed for six weeks, transition into supplementation for three weeks, then bottle-feed for the rest of the year. Other mothers breast-feed for a year, transition into supplementation with solid foods, then finish with milk given in a sippy cup. Other mothers may breast-feed for only a day, supplement for a week, and bottle-feed with formula from then on.

Even if you aren't in one of the phases, read about them all, because you'll find common issues, techniques, and tips that are useful across phases. For example, a woman going straight to bottle-feeding will still have sore breasts, an exclusively bottle-fed baby may enjoy some of the breast-feeding holds, and a breast-feeding mother who is freezing some of her breast milk will need to know about bottle-feeding.

"neh" and breast-feeding

WHEN YOU HEAR "NEH" in your baby's pre-cry, it's time to prepare to breast-feed. Allow your baby to continue making the sound while you get set up to feed.

Listen as intently as you can to the cry to help your body respond hormonally. You will notice that your breasts will start to tingle and begin to leak. This is a sign that your body is ready to feed. While you should keep track of which breast your baby last fed from, you may find that your body cues you about which breast to use for this feeding if more milk leaks from that breast.

In order to feed successfully, your baby should be calm. He can be crying, just not hysterical. If he's too upset when he starts to nurse, his little mouth will clamp down too quickly and painfully hard on your nipple, or you both may get the placement of your nipple in his mouth wrong. This can lead to the baby gulping air as he feeds, which as we will see can cause a multitude of problems later on.

If he's lying down, calm him by picking him up. Stand up, place him against your shoulder, and rock from side to side in a rhythmic way (for other calming holds and tips, see chapter 18). Remember, the calmer you are, the calmer your baby will be. Once you're both calmer, you may sit down and start to feed your baby.

Start with a comfortable position. If sitting, use a high-backed chair; if you prefer to nurse in bed, make sure you have enough pillow support for your back. You want to prevent getting a sore back, as you are likely to be in this position for a long time during a feeding. Make sure you have a side table to hold needed items, such as water, a burping cloth, lanolin ointment, nipple shields and pads, a spare bra, a book, and so on. You should be able to reach these things with minimal movement. Experiment with using several large pillows or pillows of different sizes to help support your back, your arm, and the baby. For example, a pillow under your nursing arm can be a great help in supporting your baby, leaving your other arm free to help position your little one.

There are many holds, and often it will take a few attempts to find the one that suits you and your baby best. You may also find that you prefer different holds at different times of day. For example, you may prefer a lying-down, in-bed hold for the midnight feedings, the side-football hold when your breast is a bit full, and the across-the-chest hold in a more public setting. It's a good idea to become familiar with a few different breast-feeding holds, in case your nipples get sore and you need a backup hold, or you find yourself having to nurse in an irregular situation.

Also, drink water, water, and more water! I can't stress this enough. You probably have noticed that when your breasts let down, you get incredibly thirsty. Make sure you have a few full water bottles close at hand, as drinking water helps maintain adequate fluid intake (essential when breast-feeding), *and* helps relax you when you start feeding.

three breast-feeding holds

SITTING UPRIGHT (CRADLE HOLD)

For most women, sitting upright is the most practical way to feed their baby, and it can be done anywhere.

- Find a relaxing place to sit, either in a comfortable chair that has plenty of back support, or propped up with pillows in bed. Place a pillow on your lap to help take some of the weight of your baby's body and to bring him closer to your breast.

- Cupping your breast with your fingers resting on your chest wall, underneath your breast, use your thumb to press the top of the breast slightly, modifying the breast shape and making it easier for your baby to attach to your nipple.

- Bring your baby up to your breast so his chin is against it and his tongue is underneath your nipple, supporting his bottom as well as his head and neck.

- Encourage the baby to open his mouth by touching your baby's lips with your nipple. Once his mouth is open wide, guide your nipple gently toward his mouth. Once you can see that his jaws are wide open and he has a mouthful of breast and you feel the flow from your nipple, you will know he has latched on properly. You also observe his jaw muscles working well; his temples will be moving, and he will have a firm grip on your nipple.

LYING DOWN

A lying-down position can work well, particularly for late-night or early-morning feedings, and when your baby is easily accessible from your bed. It can also be good if you have had a cesarean section or need to vary or change your nursing position to help relieve nipple soreness.

- Place your baby alongside you, with your body facing her, and support your baby's body and head with one arm. Her head should be level with your nipple. Gently roll her body to face yours. Try to avoid propping yourself up on one elbow, as this can make it difficult for your baby to latch on.

- Supporting your breast as you would if using the upright position (see above), cup your breast and use your thumb on top to modify the shape of your breast, and push your nipple into the desired position. Touch your nipple to your baby's lips to encourage her to open up. Wait until her mouth is open wide; then guide your breast toward her mouth.

- Continue to support her body and head while she is feeding. If necessary, use your elbow to slightly raise her head above her body to help with her swallowing and to reduce air intake.

BABY ALONGSIDE

I learned this position when I was nursing my son Tomas, and I later discovered that it is recommended by the World Health Organization (WHO). It works well for women in many situations: those who have twins and need to feed them together; those having difficulties with blocked ducts; women needing to use another position because of sore breasts or nipples; or those having difficulties with their baby latching on to the nipple.

- Sit comfortably in a place that has space for a pillow beside you—if sitting in a chair, it is preferable to use one without an armrest that might bang the baby's head. Use a pillow to help you support your baby's body.

- Cradling your baby with the arm closer to the breast he's about to feed on, position your baby to the side of you, with his head facing the outer side of your breast. If it is your left breast, for example, use your left arm to support your baby's head and body. Your arm and your baby's body will rest beside you rather than in front, as with other holds.

- Support your breast with your hand, modifying its shape and positioning your nipple as in the holds described above, tickling your baby's lips until he responds by opening his mouth wide. Gently guide his mouth toward your breast without leaning forward or to the side. If your baby has trouble with taking in air, you can angle his body to be lower than his head by adjusting the pillow and/or moving your elbow down.

using "neh" to know when to switch breasts

OPINIONS VARY as to which breast should be offered first, and when you should allow the baby to switch from one breast to the other. I have found that it's best to be guided by both your baby and yourself. Personally, I would first offer the breast that is leaking more. If your baby empties the first breast and wants more, she will most likely pull off and say "neh," at which point you can switch her to the other breast.

when to burp your baby

THERE IS A SCHOOL of thought that requires a mother to interrupt a baby's nursing to burp her baby before putting him back on the breast. Whenever I have seen mothers doing this, it seemed to cause more upset than benefit. The baby would become disturbed at the interruption, pulling the baby off the nipple often hurt the mother, and both baby and mother became agitated if there were latching-on problems. The happiest babies were the ones left to do what they do best—feed—and when it was time to change breasts, the baby took the lead: it happened when he chose to latch off himself. Leave the burping for after the completed feeding—or for when your baby says "eh" during a feeding (see "When 'Neh' Becomes 'Eh,'" below).

WHEN "NEH" BECOMES "EH"

Halfway through a feed, Lucy would begin pulling on and off the breast. She was clearly trying to latch on, but then would begin crying with my nipple actually in her mouth. My nipples were cracked and sore, and the whole experience of feeding was painful. Then I realized that during these times, Lucy was saying "eh." She needed to burp! I'd sit her up and help her to push out the air. Then she'd start to say "neh" again, and I'd continue feeding. My nipples are saying thank you! –JENNY

One exception to this is the "just before bed" feed, when babies often fall asleep on the breast. Then I would advise burping between breasts, only after your baby has pulled himself off. Also, hold the baby and gently pat his back for as long as possible after the completed feed.

If you have a baby who has issues with gas and wind or reflux, consider burping her before feeding. This can be done as you carry her to your nursing chair, or for a quick minute on your knee. This will help eliminate the possibility of feeding on top of an air bubble, making the feeding process smoother. Also, your baby will be less likely to pull off the breast in the midst of a feeding. Try to pick a breast-feeding hold that allows your baby's head to be elevated higher than her body, and try to spend as much time as possible burping her afterward, as well as holding her upright throughout the day, either in a sling, a BabyBjörn, or a bouncy seat. Use nursing holds that minimize wind by keeping the baby at a slight angle, with her head higher than her bottom (for more holds to help release wind or gas, see chapters 6 and 9).

have they had enough of "neh"?

ONE OF THE issues with breast-feeding is that we are never quite sure how much milk the baby is drinking or how much our breasts are producing. Here's where "neh" can come to the rescue. Since your baby will say "neh" if she's hungry, if she's still crying "neh" after her feeding, that's a good indicator that it's time to look into methods to increase your milk production. Consult your baby's pediatrician, who can check your baby's weight gain and measurements and help you to resolve your concerns. If your baby pulls off the breast and is content, then I would say she's had enough. If she pulls off and says another word like "eh" ("I need to burp"), attend to that need and then listen for whether she says "neh" again. Sometimes moving an air bubble out or just changing positions can leave some space for a top-up.

NOT ENOUGH "NEH"? WAYS
TO HELP INCREASE MILK PRODUCTION

There are lots of ways to increase milk production, and it's often most effective to try all these options.

- *First, record your baby crying the "neh" hunger sound, and listen to it often.* This will make your breasts respond. It may feel awkward when it happens, but that's simply your body responding to the sound of your hungry baby and starting to produce milk. Make sure to listen to your recording an hour and a half before a feeding is due.

- *Make sure you're drinking enough.* Sufficient quantities of fluid are essential for milk production. Keep a bottle of water with you at all times, especially when feeding, and try to drink from it as often as possible.

- *Let your baby comfort nurse as well as hunger nurse.* Also, offer a "top-off" on the last feeding of the day.

- *Offer both breasts twice.* Make sure your baby is sucking to the end of your supply and not just enjoying the quick, easy start.

- *Let your baby feed for as long as possible and try to change breasts even if the first breast isn't emptied.*

- *Maximize the opportunity for skin-to-skin contact and lots of cuddles.* Keep up the nighttime feedings and keep your baby close at hand in the same room. Carry your baby in a sling rather than putting her in a stroller or crib.

- *Take care of yourself.* Make sure you're eating a well-balanced diet (this is not the time to go on a weight-loss diet), getting enough sleep (nap when your baby naps; express some milk, and let your partner do the feeding), and minimizing outside stresses.

expressing your breast milk

SOMETIMES IT'S SIMPLY NOT PRACTICAL for us to be with our babies all the time, and we will need to express breast milk so someone else can feed them. It can be a good idea to have a few bags of breast milk put away in the freezer in case of emergencies—for example, you can't get home to feed your baby on time, or you get sick and need to take medication you don't wish your baby to ingest. Other times, it may be that our nipples weren't made for the rigors of breast-feeding or have become very sore or sensitive, and we may need to express milk by a means other than our little one's mouth. Below I've profiled the three main ways to express breast milk. A tip: when you're expressing, listen to a recording of your baby's "neh" cry. You'll be surprised how much easier and more comfortable you will find expressing.

For more information on bottle-feeding (breast milk or formula), read on.

EXPRESSING SUCCESS

I had to go back to work, so I began to express my breast milk, hoping to build a reserve. The trouble was that after feeding Nico, I didn't have much to spare. Then a girlfriend suggested freezing my milk in an ice-cube tray. That way I could store small amounts separately, and thaw out a few cubes as needed.

Once I went back to work, I took a recording of Nico crying. I would pump in my car during my lunch break, and again in the afternoon. Listening to his cry made the expressing so much easier. My breasts would let down even before I attached the pump!
—ALESSANDRA

SELF-EXPRESSING

This is a method I could never master, but I've seen many women do it. I've been told that self-expressing is less painful than a pump for those with sensitive nipples. It is much slower than using a pump, and obviously is easier if your breasts are full.

Cup your breast with your thumb on top and your forefinger under the areola. Gently massage your thumb and finger together in a forward motion. The motion is repeated rhythmically. The aim is to gently massage your whole breast, not pull on the nipple.

MANUAL PUMP

Manual pumps tend to have a bottle attached to a suction cap that fits over your nipple. You squeeze a hand mechanism to draw out the milk. It's quicker and easier than self-expressing, and like self-expressing, it's quiet, so you can use it in a more public setting. You also don't have to rely on electricity, so there's no need to hunt for a power outlet. Follow the instructions that come with your pump and remember to listen to your baby's "neh" recording.

ELECTRIC PUMP

An electric pump is fast and easy, but it's more expensive than a manual pump. However, one can often be leased from your maternity hospital or lactation clinic. Electric pumps also have been shown to increase milk production, probably because of their speed in collecting milk—perhaps your body thinks there's a very hungry child attached! Follow the instructions and don't be afraid to try a few different styles and brands.

As with any equipment, especially those associated with feeding your baby, make sure it is always clean and sterilized. Each piece of equipment will come with instructions on how to do this. Make sure to follow the directions carefully, as you certainly don't want any bacteria creeping in to make your little one sick.

Refrigerate expressed breast milk as soon as possible—the quicker the better. Breast milk can be stored at room temperature for as long as five to six hours, and in the refrigerator for up to ninety-six hours. You can freeze breast milk, and it will stay fresh for a few weeks. Freeze in small amounts, so as not to waste any once it's thawed out. It's a precious commodity! Frozen breast milk can be thawed by running the bag or bottle under lukewarm tap water and letting it sit for thirty minutes, or keeping it in the fridge, to be used within a twenty-four-hour period. Do not thaw or heat your baby's milk in the microwave, as it heats unevenly and can cause scalding of your baby's mouth.

"neh" and supplement feeding

UNTIL NOW, there has typically been a clear distinction between breast-feeding and bottle-feeding, with little advice for transitional supplementing: feeding breast milk as well as formula to the baby.

In my research around the world, supplementation is quite common. This is especially true in cultures that include multigenerational homes. A grandmother might feed her grandchild formula during the day while the baby's mother is away or working, with Mom breast-feeding at night before bed and in the morning. In more tribal settings, many women share breast-feeding duties, which I don't advise but mention here as an example of how supplementing is a long-standing custom. Even in Western cultures, before formulas were manufactured, a wet nurse might have been hired to feed during the evenings, while the mother nursed during the day.

The current all-or-nothing approach to breast-feeding limits us. Mothers who may wish to breast-feed but who can't for physical or practical reasons may not do it at all. Babies who could be receiving the benefits of breast milk miss out.

Even just a day or two of breast-feeding benefits your baby. Colostrum is the first liquid produced by the breast after the baby's birth, and it continues to be produced for a couple of days. It is full of antibodies and easy-to-digest sugars and cannot be replicated by a manufactured milk; it is also lower in fat and higher in protein than ordinary breast milk.

If you find you need to supplement in order to keep breast-feeding, do so. Breast-feeding even just once a day is a better alternative than going straight to exclusive bottle-feeding of formula.

Sometimes our bodies can't produce enough milk for our babies, and we find that our babies are still hungry even after we've tried to increase our supply. You may especially feel this in the evenings after a day of feeding has left your breasts little time to replenish. Rather than giving up on breast-feeding altogether, consult your doctor about supplemental feeding. This can complement and even strengthen your breast-feeding—for example, giving your baby a bottle in the evening to fill her tummy and get her off to sleep gives your body time to replenish your breast milk.

In these situations, it is very important to keep using the strategies for increasing your milk supply; otherwise, you may find that your supply continues to decrease, rather than staying the same.

Mothers who have good success with supplementing tend to let their babies breast-feed; then once the baby starts pulling off and crying "neh," they top him up with the bottle. The baby stays in the same hold, and the bottle nipple is simply inserted instead of the breast nipple.

Once your baby is fed and wants to comfort suck, you can offer your breast again. That way your breast still gets stimulated as much as possible, and your baby also gets his nutritional requirements. It all translates to a calmer baby, a better sleep for baby and you, and a better routine for all.

This method also gives you the option to return to exclusive breast-feeding if your milk supply increases. You'd be surprised how having a cold, not getting enough sleep, or not drinking enough water can affect your milk supply. Sometimes a baby's growth spurt demands extra milk, and your body needs a little time for your milk supply to adjust.

DECIDING TO SUPPLEMENT—AND HOW "NEH" HELPED

I had looked forward to nursing from the moment I learned I was pregnant. Even when I had problems with nursing, I persevered because I believed in it, but Hahona was crying a lot. After I learned the Dunstan Baby Language, it became clear to me that he was saying "neh" after feedings and throughout the night and day. Clearly, he was hungry.

I consulted a lactation consultant, and we agreed I didn't have enough milk to satisfy my growing baby. I decided to supplement feed, and started by adding a bottle at the end of the day, when my milk supply was lowest. Within a day, Hahona was sleeping well and had gone from being a difficult baby

*to being an angel—all because he wasn't hungry anymore.
Being able to understand his hunger word helped me make
the supplement-feeding decision together with him. To have
struggled on, not realizing he was hungry, would have been very
hard for us both and would have affected our relationship.*

—*KAHUIWI*

The studies I have conducted bear out what Kahuiwi learned:
the Dunstan Baby Language works well with both breast-feeding
and supplementation. With a clearer awareness of their baby's
hunger, mothers who didn't have enough milk were able to add a
bottle at the end of the day or slot it in instead of a feeding. (For
tips on maintaining or increasing milk production, see "Not Enough
'Neh'? Ways to Help Increase Milk Production," on page 50.)

holds for supplement feeding

SITTING UPRIGHT (CRADLE HOLD)

You can supplement feed using the standard cradle hold, where you
feed sitting up with the baby lying diagonally across your chest.
Breast-feed as normal, making sure to switch breasts to get maxi-
mum sucking on both. You will know your baby is still hungry if he
pulls off and cries "neh." Make sure it is "neh" and not "eh" (needing
to burp) or "eairh" (the word for having gas). Offer the first breast
again to make sure your baby has emptied that side. If he continues
to pull off, switch sides again. Offer each breast twice: twice on one
side, and twice on the other. This will encourage your baby to suck to
the end of your milk supply.

Once you are sure there is no milk left, slide the nipple of the bottle down your breast without moving the baby. As he starts to cry "neh," substitute the nipple of the bottle for your breast. Once the baby has finished feeding, if he seems to want to comfort suck, replace the bottle nipple with your own.

FACING OUT

I was taught this hold by a Norwegian maternity nurse. The aim is to have the bottle near you and your breasts so the baby will smell you but will have access only to a bottle, as well as to help increase your milk supply by replicating many aspects of breast-feeding: skin-to-skin contact with your baby and his smell and sounds.

Start by lying with your back propped against a pillow, your body angled at approximately 35 degrees. Place your baby with her back against your chest, making the most of skin-to-skin contact—that is, with both of your shirts off. Your baby's bottom will rest on your tummy, her head between your breasts. If it's cold, you can wrap a blanket around both of you.

Rest your elbow on the side of the mattress and place the bottle nipple into your baby's mouth, keeping the angle between the baby and the bottle at 45 degrees.

bottle-feeding

DECIDING TO BOTTLE-FEED

I had given up a lot of my medications during pregnancy because I wanted to give our baby the best start possible in life. But after the birth, I realized I also needed my health and to be present

with my baby. I decided to bottle-feed because it meant I could take the medications I needed to stay well and be a good mom.
—CATHERINE

While every effort should be made to breast-feed for as long as possible, even if it is only for the first few days or requires supplement feeding, there are many reasons why we may not be able to feed our babies our breast milk. If bottle-feeding is needed, parents should feel confident that they've done all they could to breast-feed and that they've chosen a method of feeding that suits them and their baby best. A relaxed, confident mother and a well-fed baby are always preferred over a sick or emotionally distressed parent and a poorly nourished infant. Always make this decision with input from trusted medical experts rather than from well-meaning family and friends. Once the decision has been made, feel good that you have made the right choice and concentrate on bonding with your new baby.

By listening to and understanding your infant's language, you can still feed on demand when bottle-feeding. Because "neh" helps you know when to prepare to nurse, it can be a big help to bottle-feeding parents, as there's more prep time involved.

Try to stay ahead of the game with nipple and bottle sterilization, so you can make up your baby's formula without having to fuss with sterilizing. Remember to use a thermometer to test the formula temperature, and never use the microwave to heat your baby's bottle. When making up the formula, follow the manufacturer's instructions exactly, without exception.

bottle-feeding holds

MANY OF THE BREAST-FEEDING HOLDS are perfectly suited to bottle-feeding. Your aim is to replicate the physical and emotional experience of breast-feeding as much as possible, to help with bonding and to help your child feel attached to you.

Pick up your baby each time you feed; cradle her, and have it be a special time for the two of you. Even when your baby is older, avoid propping the bottle or holding it while she lies in a crib. Use this time to connect with your little one. You are replacing only the source of the milk, not the rest of the feeding experience—and you're certainly not replacing *you*! Your baby wants to smell you and be held by you during feeding, and you can provide that just as well with a bottle as with a breast.

Have a designated chair or place for feedings, and keep it comfortable for you as well as for your baby by using cushions to support your holds and your back. If you had a cesarean or are still lactating, your body may still feel uncomfortable, so be gentle with yourself. Remember to keep necessities in easy reach while feeding: things such as water, a burping cloth, pacifier, a change of bra or breast pads (yes, your breasts may still leak), and any other items you may need.

SITTING UPRIGHT (CRADLE HOLD)

For most women, sitting upright is the most practical way to feed their baby. It's also a hold that can be done anywhere.

- Find a comfortable place to sit upright, either in a high-backed chair that has plenty of back support, or propped up with pillows in bed.
- Place a pillow on your lap.
- Cradle your baby in one arm, with the back of his neck in the crook of your arm, and rest your arm on the pillow on your lap. Keep your baby's head angled above his body at all times.
- Have your baby open his mouth by touching his lips with the bottle nipple. Once his mouth is open wide, guide the nipple into his mouth. Make certain that the nipple is all the way in your baby's mouth, on top of his tongue, so he'll suck in as little air as possible.
- Keep the bottle at a 45-degree angle. When he starts to finish, tip the bottle so he doesn't gulp in any excess air.

LYING DOWN

A lying-down position can work well, particularly for late-night or early-morning feedings, and when your baby is easily accessible from your bed. It can also be good if you have had a cesarean or need another position to help relieve breast soreness (even if you're not breast-feeding, you will still be sore for a while).

- Place your baby alongside you with your body facing him. Support your baby's head in the crook of your arm with his body angled down onto the mattress.
- Make sure you are comfortable.

- Touch the bottle nipple to your baby's lips to encourage him to open up. Wait until his mouth is open wide, then guide the bottle nipple into his mouth.
- Continue to support his body and head while he is feeding. If necessary, use your elbow to slightly raise his head above his body to help with his swallowing and to reduce air intake.
- Remember to keep the bottle at a 45-degree angle.

BABY PROPPED AGAINST YOUR KNEES

This is a method often used in Turkey, Pakistan, and India (they tend to swaddle young babies beforehand; see chapter 5). It is good for babies with colic or reflux, or these who say "eh" and "eairh" (those who have to burp or pass gas) frequently.

- While sitting in bed or lying on the couch or the floor, place some cushions under your knees to elevate them so they're at about a 30-degree angle.
- Place your baby on your lap, propped up against your knees, with your baby's bottom resting on your tummy.
- Rest your elbow on your hip for support and to help keep the bottle at a 45-degree angle.
- Guide the bottle nipple into your baby's mouth.

This position can be tiring for your arms, so it's important to keep the bottle angled correctly. The plus to this method is that it helps reduce the baby's air intake and facilitates a lot of eye contact between you and your baby.

important tips for formula feeding

FIRST, YOU MUST USE a specially designed formula for newborn babies. Never give babies younger than twelve months milk intended for adults, no matter what type—goat, cow, soy, powdered, or condensed.

If you're using formula from the very start, be sure to bring some to the hospital, and practice sterilizing the bottles and making up the formula in advance.

If at all possible, try to breast-feed your newborn for at least the first few days, or for as many days as you can, so that she can get the benefit of the colostrum, which contains important antibodies not found elsewhere. If you are unable to do this, speak to your doctor about some alternatives.

There are many different formulas on the market today, some milk based, some soy based, and others based on something else entirely. Your lactation expert and/or your doctor will know what type suits your needs best and which is best for your baby. It may be that you'll start with a cow-based formula, especially for a newborn baby. As a general rule, soy-based formulas should be used only on the advice of your doctor. As I work with babies who cry a lot, I tend to favor the low-allergy, low-lactose, high-protein formulas for colicky, reflux-prone, or allergic babies. For the typical baby with no immediate health concerns, start with a cow-based formula specific for the age of your baby.

Try to buy a high-quality formula as close to human milk as possible. Don't be surprised if you don't find the right formula on the first try; you may need to switch a couple of times to get just the right one. Always do this with your doctor's help, and come prepared with questions and answers for your baby's appointment. Finally, always follow the "make up" instructions exactly—diluting or strengthening the formula can cause feeding problems for your infant.

ALLERGY CONCERNS

There are specialty formulas designed to minimize reactions in babies with a family history of allergies, such as asthma, hay fever, eczema, and nut and soy allergies. It's especially important to try to breast-feed if your family has a history of allergies. Babies with allergies do best when exclusively breast-fed for four to six months, but when this is impossible, a specialty formula is needed, often prescription based. Your doctor can advise you on these formulas.

BABY LANGUAGE AND FORMULA ALLERGIES

My third child would scream about an hour after feedings—and I mean really scream. She would pull up her legs, screw up her face, and I could just tell there was something very wrong. Even her stools looked unusual. I had learned about baby cries from seeing Priscilla Dunstan on television, and I recognized that when my daughter cried after feedings, she was making the sound that said she had lower-intestinal gas. I took her to the pediatrician and we changed to a low-lactose formula. That did the trick! Within a few days she was fine. —TOBY

THE RIGHT BOTTLE AND NIPPLE

Latex, rubber, plastic, glass; fast flow, slow flow . . . the choices are endless. There are bottles that supposedly reduce colic, bottles claimed to replicate the breast nipple exactly, and bottles purported to benefit tooth development. Whew!

My advice is to start with a few different types of basic bottles and nipples specifically designed for the age of your baby, and then experiment. If you're planning on supplemental feeding, try a wide nipple, as this is more like the breast and will help with the transitions between breast and bottle.

Once you find the type of nipple your baby prefers, you can then work out which bottle suits him best. Again, this is a bit of a trial-and-error process, but there are some guidelines I've seen help new mothers:

- If your baby is a windy baby, that is, a baby who says "eh" (see chapters 3 and 6) or "eairh" frequently (see chapters 7 and 9), opt for the colic-reduction designs—some of them really work.
- If your baby says "neh" most often, opt for a regular, easy-flow design.
- If your baby falls asleep quickly and immediately after a feed, or if "owh" is his most frequent reflex cry, then use a bent-shape bottle, which helps to lessen the amount of air the baby takes in and also allows you to adjust the bottle without moving your baby too much.

For moms who are pumping, often the pump will have bottle attachments, which make it easier to collect and refrigerate breast milk without constantly having to transfer milk from one container to another.

BOTTLE-FEEDING PROBLEMS

If your baby pulls off the bottle but says "neh" and there's still milk in the bottle, check for a blockage in the nipple. Sometimes, undissolved formula can clog the nipple, making it hard for your baby to get the milk at the right flow. Simply squeeze or suck the nipple end to clear the blockage, or replace the nipple with another and offer it to your baby again.

If your baby has finished the bottle but still says "neh," chances are your baby wants more. This increase in appetite can be brought on by basic development or a growth spurt, or may simply occur as the baby gets older.

With this method of demand bottle-feeding, you may find that your baby wants different amounts at different times of day. Just like a breast-fed baby, a bottle-fed baby has different energy needs at different times.

If your baby pulls off the bottle and says "eh," then it's time to burp him and listen for the "neh" that will follow if he wants to continue to feed.

THE WRONG FORMULA?

If you find that your baby is displaying signs of discomfort, such as long bouts of crying, pulling her legs up, or making "eairh" sounds (see chapter 7) mixed with "heh" (see chapter 8), or if she is gassier or spitting up frequently, you may need to rethink the formula. Consult your doctor about trying another type. Make sure you keep a diary of when you fed your baby, how much she ate, how the feeding went (smoothly, as in not pulling on or off the nipple? gulping or crying during the feeding? fussy? gassy?), how soon after the feeding any crying or cramping started, and any other behavioral details you think could help your doctor work out what the issue is. It may be a developmental issue, a handling issue, colic, reflux, or a need to change the formula. By keeping a diary, you can help your doctor determine with you the right choice for your baby.

CHAPTER 5

"owh" solutions

MAKING SENSE OF SLEEP

"Owh" is the word we hear the most often from our daughter, probably because sleep is our biggest issue. I think it sort of sounds like a cat, but my husband thinks it sounds more like when you stub your toe! Either way, it is a definite "owh" sound. Her mouth is in a yawn shape when she makes that sound in her cry—which makes perfect sense, since we all yawn when we're tired! –ANNE

When you hear "owh" within your baby's cry, you will know your baby is tired. This is the time to get her ready for bed.

your baby's sleep

IT'S IMPORTANT TO BE ADAPTABLE in your approach to nighttime sleep, as parenting doesn't end when the sun goes down. Just as we don't ignore our baby's needs during the day, so we shouldn't be ignoring our baby's needs at night.

Have realistic expectations about newborn sleep. A newborn is not going to sleep through the night. You are going to be sleep deprived, and there will be moments when you wonder if this will never end. It will, and it's only for a few months that you will need to be patient and help your baby learn the skill of sleeping through the night. Try not to be frustrated when it seems he will never fall asleep. Make the most of the "owh" sound, and be ready when you hear it. Remember to be calm, and ask for help if you find you need a break.

That said, newborns actually sleep a lot—typically sixteen to seventeen hours a day. Unfortunately, that sleep is spread throughout the day and night in bursts, anywhere from ten to fifteen minutes, to two to four hours. This means interrupted sleep for the parents, so consider taking naps throughout the day.

your sleep

CONSIDER YOUR OWN NEEDS
AS WELL AS YOUR BABY'S
Originally we started with our daughter sleeping in her own room, but as the days went on and the lack of sleep caught up with us, we ended up moving her crib into our room. It made it easier for me to hear her cry and to quickly get up to feed and change her. —TERRY

No one really knows what it's like to be sleep deprived until they are! Sleep deprivation is very real for new parents, and symptoms include irritability, lack of concentration, forgetfulness, mood swings, erratic behavior, and sadness. When there is a baby in the house who isn't sleeping well, it affects everyone, and it may take some time to reverse the effects. Everyone—baby and you—will need to catch up on sleep.

Be flexible and consider not only your baby's needs but also your own. Often parents find that they need to change their approach as they go along. Don't worry about this; you are gaining information each day about your baby, and this new information will help you make the best decision that suits you and your family.

If you're feeling at wits' end over sleep, take a few days and make sleep your priority. Listen closely for your baby's "owh," forget all the household chores, and sleep when your baby sleeps. The good news is that babies don't stay this way, and sometime between four and six months, you can look forward to a good stretch of eight (or even up to twelve) hours of sleep at night.

Knowing to listen for "owh" makes a difference in more areas than just sleeping. There is a real halo effect from having a well-rested baby. Being tired affects all parts of life, and for a newborn baby it can mean the difference between being able to cope and not being able to. Parents often find that once the sleep issues have been resolved, their baby also feeds more easily and plays more comfortably. Interaction becomes a joy, as it is easier to bond with a happy baby than one who is tired and upset.

This benefit transfers to us as parents as well. If your baby is getting more sleep, chances are you are, too. Our self-esteem as parents also increases, as we feel we're more in tune with our baby's needs. It is truly a virtuous cycle that improves simply with more sleep—and more sleep occurs with early detection of "owh."

SOLVING "OWH": TEACHING SLEEP

Even though knowing when your baby's body is tired will make your job of helping her to sleep much easier, recognizing this magic word won't eliminate the need to comfort your baby and teach her how to sleep. Sleeping, like being awake, requires learned skills and habits. Just as we parent and teach our little ones during the day, so too we parent at night:

- We want to encourage our baby to learn the difference between night sleep and day sleep.
- We want our baby to be able to wake up and feel comfortable enough to fall back asleep.
- We want our baby to think of her bed as a safe sanctuary that comforts and recharges her rather than as a place where she feels afraid and alone.

A going-to-sleep routine is an important part of teaching sleep. In fact, you can make slight variations in the routine to signal to your child whether this is:

- a long nighttime sleep,
- a daytime nap, or
- a go-back-to-sleep time.

How you put your baby to sleep at each of these key moments will teach her what's expected and prepare her for what's coming next. For example, a nighttime feeding done in low light, with limited eye contact and a quick, no-nonsense diaper change, would (in time) signal to your baby "nighttime, go back to sleep." On the other hand, a gentle rock and being placed in a crib in the living room might signal a nap. A bath, followed by a massage, a song, and bottle or breast would signal a long, nighttime sleep.

Any routine works better if it's based on you and your baby's preferences and done when the baby is tired and saying "owh." This will cause the least amount of stress for all concerned. It's much easier to work with a contented, well-rested baby than with an overtired, anxious one. (That goes for parents, too!) For more tips on starting a routine, see part 3.

"OWH" AND BETTER SLEEP FOR YOUR BABY

Being able to hear when your baby's body is ready for sleep frees you from battling with a child who is either overtired or not yet tired. As we ourselves know, if we go to bed when we feel tired, we often have no problem falling asleep. However, on the nights when we delay ("Just one more chapter," or "I'll just unload the dishwasher"), we find we're no longer tired when we've finished. Most of us have also experienced those nights, perhaps around the change to daylight savings or when we travel across time zones, when we want to fall asleep, but our body won't let us. There's a reason why sleeping pills are a multibillion-dollar industry!

Our babies have less control over their worlds, lower sleep reserves, and less experience with sleeping habits—so how could a one-week-old possibly get it right? If we as adults have problems sleeping, we need to be realistic about our children.

Sleep cannot be forced; it is a state that comes on naturally. If you're not hearing the "owh" sound, then chances are your baby isn't tired yet. That said, the calmer and the more relaxed your baby is, the easier it will be for him to feel his fatigue and begin saying the "owh" word.

Once you hear "owh," then it's time to be quick and do the settling techniques to help him fall asleep feeling safe, secure, and loved.

"Owh" can also clue you in to your baby's unique body rhythms

71

and needs. If you have other children, you'll find your baby's rhythms may be totally different from her siblings' when they were her age.

DIFFERENT BABY, DIFFERENT PATTERNS

Christopher, my first child, was easy to put to sleep. I would feed him, change his diaper, give him a gentle rock, and he was out. But when Annabelle was born, I spent hours trying to get her to fall asleep. After learning the sounds, I discovered that Annabelle's pattern was different. When she cried a few hours after eating, she was tired, not hungry. And she wanted to feed after a nap, not before. Trying to feed a sleepy baby is hard; trying to get an awake baby to sleep is even harder! Now I put Annabelle to bed when I hear her saying "owh." The process is much easier. It's a complete flip from what I did with Christopher, but I guess each child is different, and the only way we know is by listening to them. —SALLY

WAITING FOR THAT LAST "OWH"

The bedtime routine is one that ends the day and settles your child to sleep for a long stretch. There are generally a number of things that make this sleep different from the other, shorter naps. It is a routine that relaxes your baby, makes sleep attractive, and signals that sleep is expected. Parents often think that babies should automatically become quiet at nighttime. But since sleep is a learned skill, we need to show as much patience and understanding with our baby's nighttime learning as we do during the day.

Even once you have a routine, it is best to wait until your baby is saying "owh," so be flexible. You might need to cuddle a few more minutes, or cut it short by a few. Let it happen. Babies (and adults, too) learn better in a relaxed, receptive state. Remember also that babies operate on primal survival instincts that we don't fall asleep if we feel we are at risk. Thus, the safer and more secure we can make our babies feel, the more easily they will fall asleep and stay asleep.

"OWH" AND THE NIGHTTIME ROUTINE

"I had a lot of trouble getting Prudence to sleep. She would have crying fits, and her movements would become jerky. I knew she was tired, so I would rock her, put her in the stroller, and even put her in the car and drive around the block to get her to sleep. It was a never-ending issue, and I knew there must be a better way. Now that I know about the meaning of the different cries, I act as soon as I hear the word 'owh.' I wrap her up, pop in the pacifier, and tuck her into bed—and she goes instantly to sleep. Not a cry, not a scream. Out like a light! If I miss the cue though, she gets very upset with crying, and we end up back where we were—with never-ending car rides." —TONY

first things first: where will your baby sleep?

WHERE OUR BABIES WILL SLEEP is often dictated by our cultural beliefs and comfort level. Wherever you choose to have your new baby sleep, make sure to provide the safest environment possible. Be aware of the risk of SIDS (sudden infant death syndrome) and what you can do to help prevent it from happening, including:

- Always place your baby on his back to sleep.
- Keep the crib free of excess bedding or bedding that could cover the baby's face if he were to move.
- Keep toys outside the crib, especially stuffed toys.
- Make sure to keep the baby's room temperature even.
- Don't allow anyone to smoke anywhere near your infant.
- Do your best to avoid excess crying and stress in your baby.

As your baby gets older, he will tend to roll and move about. Make sure you keep the sides up on the crib, tuck any bedclothes in tightly, and don't leave your baby on an adult bed or sofa without a side grid to protect him from rolling off.

Below are some of the main ways parents choose to have their babies sleep, but there are as many variations as there are babies. Choose one that suits you and your baby's needs and makes you comfortable. Both you and your baby have a lot to learn in the next few months, so be gentle with both your baby and yourself.

CO-SLEEPING

It can be a bit dangerous to co-sleep with a very small and helpless baby. Better to keep his bassinet or crib next to the bed, or to use a co-sleeper that straps to the side of the bed. This allows you to hear your baby's sounds and to reach out a hand to him if necessary, without the risk of hurting him. Remember, sleep deprivation is a big issue for parents of newborns, and safety needs to be considered. When you finally do get to sleep, you may not wake up as easily as you think!

SAME ROOM, DIFFERENT BED

Same-room sleeping—when the baby sleeps in her own crib, located in the parents' room or just outside it—seems to be the most popular with parents and newborn babies. Parents can easily hear the baby's sounds and are able to get up quickly, but they have a little privacy. There is no danger of rolling on the baby or risk that the baby's cries will go unheard for long. With those babies who are never happy unless they're being held, swaddling can help (see "Swaddling," page 81).

SEPARATE BEDROOMS

DREAMS VERSUS REALITY

I had dreams of co-sleeping with my baby, but he was just so noisy! Every time he sniffed I would wake up and be scared he wasn't well. And the snoring! Who would have thought a baby would snore? —EMILY

Separate bedrooms is a very Western way of sleeping, but it is much preferred by some parents. Babies are not as quiet as you may think! They snore and snuffle and cry out in their sleep, making it hard for some parents to sleep. Using a baby monitor can help—although you will still hear your child, it may not be quite as disturbing. A separate room does require you to fully get out of bed and go to the baby's room when needed. It also may mean that you miss your baby's pre-cry sound for hunger and that your baby may wake more fully when hungry. But parents who choose this method may find that the benefit of better sleep outweighs the extra time they may spend settling their baby and themselves for sleep.

falling-asleep techniques

PARENT SOOTHING

I used this technique with my son and I don't regret it. Simply put, you rock or hold your baby in your arms until he falls asleep. There was something so sweet about watching my son fall asleep in my arms and being able to look down on an angel, especially as he was such a vocal, boisterous fellow when awake! The trick was that I had to put him down in his crib fairly soon after he fell asleep. Since babies spend more time than adults in the lighter stage of sleep known as the REM cycle—which is easier to wake from than deeper stages of sleep—I didn't want to risk waking him after he'd entered his REM cycle.

Parent soothing can be done in many different positions: the upright position for gassy babies or babies who are getting sleepy but haven't burped yet, the across-the-arm method for colicky babies, and the very natural rocking side-to-side method. This last method is comforting for some babies, but others can find it overwhelming.

One important trick is to resist staring at your baby until he has fallen asleep, as often the visual contact with you can keep him awake.

Another great trick, taught to me in the maternity ward by a fabulous nurse, was invaluable for my son. I would gently run my hand down his forehead and over his nose, covering his eyes. This very gentle motion encouraged him to close his eyes, and once his eyes were closed, he was off to sleep.

"OWH" AND THE GENTLE "TEACH TO SLEEP" METHOD

This method hinges on waiting until your baby is nearly—but not completely—asleep. Just before your baby falls asleep, you tuck her into bed. This approach helps your baby learn to put herself to sleep, which is necessary for being able to sleep through the night, without the harshness of leaving her to cry herself to sleep.

When using the "teach to sleep" method with "owh," you start your bedtime routine and settling techniques near your baby's typical bedtime. However, you wait until you hear "owh" to finish up. At this point, quickly finish your routine, and before the baby starts crying in earnest, wrap up the baby and place her on her back, in her crib.

She will fuss a bit, so stay close by and reassure her with a gentle rub or pat. Then, just before she falls asleep, stop the soothing techniques, so she will fall asleep on her own.

As your baby gets older, you can let her become more independent about falling asleep by stopping the soothing techniques earlier and lengthening the time she is on her own before falling asleep.

WEARING YOUR BABY

This method is ideal for many different types of infants: those who have a lot of colic or reflux; who say "eh" (need to burp) or "eairh" (need to pass gas) regularly; who fall asleep before being burped; who seem to regularly wake twenty minutes after falling asleep, crying "eh."

This technique involves the use of a sling or baby carrier. Choose the upright version for babies with gas or reflux, and the sideward version for babies who have trouble falling asleep. When it's time for sleep, you wear your baby in the sling or carrier until he's asleep, and then place him in his crib. If this sounds tricky, it can be—but don't worry, as I'll share an "old pro" way of doing it.

Start by leaning forward over the crib mattress, holding the baby (and sling) close to your chest. Once your baby's back is on the mattress, undo the carrier or sling and slide it out from underneath your baby. Gently pull away, while replacing the feel of your body with a folded blanket or small pillow on her chest. Give the baby a moment to settle; then slowly remove the blanket or pillow, pulling up the bedclothes. Remember to remove the extra pillow or blanket from the sleeping area, as well as the carrier or sling. The trick is to use whatever is at hand to substitute for the feeling of your body, so the baby isn't startled awake. It may sound complicated, but it can be done very quickly and becomes automatic.

ROCKING OR WALKING

There are many items that can help you get your baby to sleep: rockers, swings, cribs that swing, and strollers with attachable cribs that allow you to walk your baby to sleep. You probably need to try a few of them to find the right choice.

For a baby who is easily excited but slow to wind down, a change in temperature, air, or environment can be just the thing to change her focus to sleep. If this seems to be your baby's preferred method, make sure you have a stroller that has a suitable sleeping area. As mentioned, there are many models that have sleeping attachments or cribs, and these come with a suitable mattress and lowering mechanism so your baby can lie flat. Car seats and strollers are not advisable for long or regular sleeping, as they can harm your baby's developing body.

If your baby is one who needs special handling before sleep, it's particularly important that you listen carefully for "owh" and catch it in the pre-cry stage. This will make it easier for you to get your baby to sleep before she gets worked up. You may even find you no longer need to change environments.

SOUND CUES

A baby's ears start to hear twelve weeks before birth, so she will be familiar with the sounds of her environment. Once your baby is saying "owh" and you have her dressed for bed, use this to your advantage by creating a sound trigger. It could be singing a lullaby or playing classical music as she drifts off. As the baby gets older and becomes more able to fall asleep herself, you will be able to play the music to help signal that it's bedtime.

Sometimes your baby may find it hard to sleep because life is *too* quiet. Babies are actually used to quite a noisy environment. Being inside Mom's body wasn't at all quiet: her heartbeat, digestion, and respiratory systems were all rather loud! Experiment with white noise, or make a recording of something rhythmical like your dryer running. You may also find that experimenting with where the baby sleeps can work wonders, as some babies will prefer to sleep in the living room, with all the noise and activity, while others need a quiet environment to have a peaceful sleep.

what about leaving the baby to "cry it out"?

I HAVE BEEN VOCAL in my objections to leaving babies to cry until they fall asleep, or "cry it out," and indeed, the latest research suggests that excessive crying contributes to SIDS. However, every circumstance is different, and if you believe this method is right for your family, please be sure the baby is saying the "I'm tired" cry, "owh," before starting. Leaving a baby who is tired alone to fall asleep is one thing; it's quite another to leave one who is hungry, gassy, or in pain. Pediatricians worldwide advise against leaving young babies under five to six months to cry to sleep.

BABY LANGUAGE AND
THE "CRY TO SLEEP" METHOD
My mother-in-law is a big believer in the "cry to sleep" method, and after I had Elle, she came to help me. I never felt comfortable with closing the door on Elle when she cried. It just didn't feel right, but I couldn't give a reason for why. After hearing what the cries meant, I can hear that there are times when she's still hungry or has gas, and this is why she isn't sleepy. No amount of leaving her alone is going to fix those things! Now I feel more confident in disagreeing with my mother-in-law. —NANCY

methods for comforting your baby

BEING A NEW BABY in a new world can be overwhelming. While we as parents would like to be able to comfort our babies on our own, sometimes we need help.

PACIFIERS
Many babies I've worked with like to fall asleep sucking on something. If this is your baby, he may start to suck while crying "owh."

This produces a sound somewhere between "neh" and "owh," something like "owhnuh." The "owh" sound, however, will be very clear and repeated, whereas the "nuh" will sound more like a by-product.

If you hear this sound, grab the pacifier and start the settling process. If you're waiting for your milk to come in, want to increase your milk production, or even just want to maintain your milk while supplement feeding, let your little one suck on you instead of on the pacifier. Some babies will fall asleep on the breast or bottle, as having a full tummy and being in their most comfortable place are irresistibly soothing. The trick is to make sure the baby has had a full meal before bed, as you don't want him waking in an hour from hunger.

Even more important, if your baby falls asleep on you, don't get carried away adoring him! Time is of the essence. You need to get him to his sleeping place before he's heavily asleep. If he was feeding, carry him to his bed upright, gently rubbing his back in an upward motion to help any burps come out. If your baby always falls asleep after a feeding, consider a crib with a slightly elevated head, as it may help the baby burp without waking.

SWADDLING

The startle reflex can often cause a baby to involuntarily waken. Having him wrapped or swaddled can help limit that startle/wake pattern and help your baby feel more secure. As comforting as swaddling may be, though, some babies don't like to be wrapped too tightly, or they prefer to have one arm free so they can suck their fingers, or they like to have their legs free to be pulled up. Colicky babies or babies who say "eh" or "eairh" regularly tend to like the latter option, with their tummies wrapped tightly but their legs free to move. Experiment to find the right method.

To swaddle:

- Start with a small square blanket or a cheesecloth square.
- Lay it flat and fold one corner down toward its opposite corner. Depending on the size of the blanket and the size of the baby you're swaddling, the corners might meet, or your folded-down corner might be several inches short of the opposite corner. Experiment and you'll soon find what works.
- Place your baby on the turned-down flap.
- Pull one side across the middle of your baby, tucking it under his body.
- Bring the other across in the opposite direction, wrapping it around your baby's body.
- Gently lifting your baby, tuck the bottom tail under your baby.
- You can adapt this simple wrap to make it tighter or looser, leave one or both arms free, tuck up the tail loosely, or leave it untucked so she can kick her legs.

helping your baby to stay asleep

UNDERSTANDING "OWH" VS. "EH" MAKES ALL THE DIFFERENCE

James often fell asleep in the stroller or just on his own in the high chair. The problem was, he never stayed asleep. Within ten or fifteen minutes, he'd wake up screaming. I would check his diaper, offer him a feed, but nothing seemed to soothe him.

*Once I realized he was saying "eh" and had wind, I just picked him up, patted him on the back, waited until he burped, put him back down, and off to sleep he'd go again. I couldn't believe how easy it was. He's getting so much more sleep—and I've got time to do things around the house. —*KELLY

For many parents, it's not helping their baby fall asleep that's difficult but rather helping him stay asleep. For one thing, when they're first born, babies don't know the difference between night and day, and in my experience, it seems that newborns are more often awake at night. I wondered whether there was any correlation between babies' nighttime wakefulness and the timing of their movements in utero. So I asked a group of expectant moms to keep a diary of their babies' movements during the day and night during their pregnancies. After their babies were born, I asked them to track their newborns' sleeping patterns. It turned out that in utero, the babies kicked mostly at night or when their moms were resting. Some experts believe that when a pregnant mom is resting, she simply notices the baby's movements more, but I think it has something to do with motion. When we're walking around doing things, we are essentially "rocking" the unborn baby, which they find soothing. It would be natural that when a pregnant mom is sleeping or sitting still, the fetus wakes up. This may also account for why newborns are so awake at night—you might say they have a newborn version of jet lag, and need time to adjust to life on earth, no longer in utero. As your newborn gets over her jet lag, needing to be fed every three to four hours at first, you as a parent will have quite a job to help her stay asleep and learn about night sleeping and about shorter daytime sleeps.

Also, scientists have shown that a baby's sleep cycles are shorter than an adult's and that they spend more time in the lighter stage of sleep called the REM cycle. This is believed to be necessary to keep up with the extraordinary development that occurs in both body and brain. Unfortunately, one wakes from REM-cycle sleep more easily, so any disturbance such as a noise, a wet diaper, a change in temperature, or a light turning off can wake a baby.

HEARING "EH" OR "EAIRH" AFTER "OWH"

When a baby goes to sleep peacefully and then wakes up crying fifteen to twenty minutes later, chances are he has a gas issue. This often happens when babies have fallen asleep while feeding and were unable to burp properly, or if they're prone to having gas. We talked in chapter 3 about how babies—especially newborns—are not able to burp themselves. An air bubble can cause real discomfort.

Listen to the sound your baby is making. If you hear an "eh," pick him up and burp him. It's best if you can catch this in the pre-cry stage, before he's fully awake and gets agitated. If you catch the problem early, you should be able to simply pick him up, burp him over your shoulder or against your chest, and once the gas comes up, put him back down to sleep. Try to perform this quickly and quietly. If you keep the baby up too long for the burp, he will begin to say "owh," showing that he is tired, and will need to be helped to fall back to sleep.

HEARING "NEH" DURING SLEEP

If your baby half wakes from sleep and during the pre-cry says a singular "neh," but it is clear that she's still very sleepy, you can use a pacifier to soothe her back to sleep. This is very common for babies who fall asleep sucking on something: they reach the end of their sleep cycle and wake up halfway, and automatically start to suck to soothe themselves back to sleep. If your baby is young, she won't be able to find the pacifier, so a quick "pick up and drop in" will do the trick. If your baby is hungry, she will not hesitate to spit out the pacifier, waking up and clearly saying "neh, neh, neh."

THE NIGHTTIME DIAPER CHANGE

The nighttime diaper change is a parent favorite. Babies get upset when they are wet. Your baby's cry may signal her discomfort with "heh," "heheheh," or "heir" (see chapter 8).

The change is best done with a minimum of fuss. Change her, give her a pat, and put her back down to sleep if she's saying "owh" or if it is nighttime. With a boy baby, make sure that his penis is facing downward when you put his diaper on him for the night. During the day, this doesn't matter as much, but when he urinates while lying on his back, as he will at night, the urine will soak the top of the diaper and his pajamas, requiring a clothing change, too—making the process potentially more disruptive and perhaps wakening your baby more than either of you would like.

CHAPTER 6

"eh" solutions

E H" IS THE WORD you will hear in your baby's cry when she needs to burp. "Eh" is caused by reflexes in the stomach and esophagus that work together to push air out through the mouth. Because babies have limited mobility, it's important to help them relieve this complaint, as an accumulation of air bubbles makes for a very uncomfortable (and fussy!) baby.

When you hear your baby saying, "eh," act on it. I have had so many parents tell me that once they got their baby's wind situation under control, their babies fed better, slept better, and were generally more relaxed. Often the whole relationship between baby and parents changes.

THE BABY'S NOT GRUMPY . . . HE HAS GAS!

Jake has settled down so much since we started burping him when we hear "eh." It makes it very easy to know what's wrong. Now when I put him to bed, I know that he may need me to pick him up again and burp him before he'll go to sleep. Or, if he's playing on the rug and he suddenly starts to cry, it's often an "eh" cry, and I can pick him up, carry him upright for a bit while patting his back, and then put him back down—and he goes back to playing happily. Before I knew the sounds, I thought he was just a grumpy baby, but he isn't—he just has more wind than most. —SHARON

If wind is a concern, or if your baby suffers from colic or reflux, it becomes even more important to burp him every time you hear "eh," even if it's before a feed. Get into the habit of burping your baby every time you pick him up. It will make life with a windy baby much easier. Increase his upright time, and do your best to carry or wear him more often. When I studied infant cries in different cultures, I was struck that the instance of colic and reflux were significantly lower in cultures in which mothers strap babies upright against their bodies. Our more Western way of putting the baby down in a crib or stroller seems to produce more wind. In places like Bali, parents don't believe in letting their baby's feet touch the ground until the age of six months. Until then, the baby is held by the family, either in slings or in their arms. I have noticed huge improvements with windy babies whose parents changed to using slings. We'll talk more about these options in this chapter.

I have found that parents new to the Dunstan Language System usually need several days of being very conscious about the "eh" sound and concentrating on just burping and keeping their baby elevated. After that, it seems that their babies' digestion tract becomes clearer, and then they can go back to a more normal routine of just listening and burping as a way of maintenance.

techniques and tips for solving "eh"

BELOW ARE SOME WAYS to help your baby bring up the wind that's causing her to say "eh." Experiment and let your own experience and your baby guide you. You will find that, in time, you'll develop a burping routine unique to you and your baby. This routine will become second nature in helping your baby get rid of air bubbles.

BURPING AGAINST YOUR CHEST

Often simply picking up your baby and holding her upright against you can help bring up the smaller air bubbles. To improve upon this, simply start patting or rubbing your baby's back in an upward motion. Some tips:

- Cradle her bottom with your forearm.
- Let your baby's head nestle against your shoulder.
- Gently pat her back; being aware that some milk may come up, drape a burp cloth over your shoulder.
- You can stand or walk with your baby in this position. If you're standing, try rocking back and forth with one foot in front of the other.

If it's been an hour or longer since your baby's last feeding, then you have more options for addressing "eh."

BURPING UPRIGHT ON YOUR KNEE

This gentle method is good for new babies, babies who tend to spit up a lot after a feeding (other methods such as over-the-shoulder may make such babies more likely to throw up), and for parents who may not yet be confident enough with their new baby to have him over their shoulder.

- Hold the baby in a sitting position on your knee, with your baby facing to the side of you.

- It's important to hold your baby's head by placing your dominant hand on his chest so that your thumb and forefinger can prevent his head from falling forward.
- Then simply either pat or rub his back. Many parents report that patting or rubbing in an upward direction helps; others prefer a simple pat.

TILTING

- Hold the baby in a sitting position on your knee, with your baby facing to the side of you.
- It's important to hold your baby's head by placing your dominant hand on her chest, so that your thumb and forefinger can prevent her head from falling forward.
- Carefully tip your baby forward, gently doubling her over, supporting her chest as described above as you do so.
- Then, just as gently, tilt your baby backward to lie nearly flat across your knee, supporting her body with your hand on her back as you do so.
- Make sure your hand is on your baby's chest and support her body as you do this movement.
- Do this movement slowly and remember to always support her head under her chin.

ROTATION

This method uses the baby's own weight to, in effect, squish the air out.

- Place your baby sitting on your knee facing outward, with her back against your tummy. Your baby's body will be leaning into yours in a somewhat curled position, and you can help by supporting her with one hand against her trunk.

- Place your other hand under her chin to support her neck and head.
- With your whole body, gently rotate by leaning back, moving to the right, then moving forward toward the left and back to your starting point again, making sure to hold your baby's body against yours so that she rotates with you.
- This rotation, added to the weight of the baby's own stomach and her upright position, will be sure to bring up any excess air in a gentle way. If you do this after a feeding, make sure you keep a burp cloth handy. You might place it in the palm of the hand that supports the baby's neck and chin, or just keep it on the table beside you.

When your baby is older, you can rotate her on your knee without rotating your own body:

- Seat your baby on your lap, positioned as described above.
- Support her chin by cupping it in your palm.
- Lean her forward slightly.
- Ever so gently, move her body counterclockwise.
- Do that slowly for about a minute; then rotate her clockwise.

CHANGING BURPING TECHNIQUES AS YOU GO

Combining the burping methods can have a great effect, too. Make sure to transition between methods slowly and calmly until the air bubble comes up. For example:

- Pick up your baby and walk around holding her against your chest as you pat her back. Then . . .
- Sit down and seat her sideways across your knee, rubbing her back in an upward motion. Then . . .
- While in that position, tilt her forward and back a few times, making sure to keep your hands under her chin and back to support her. Then . . .
- Pat her back some more, followed by a few rotation moves. Then . . .
- Put her up against your shoulder and pat her back with the palm of your hand.

USING A PACIFIER

When you've been trying to help your baby get out a stubborn burp, adding a pacifier can sometimes help move the air up and out. The pacifier works best when the baby is up against your chest, or with the over-the-shoulder burping method (see "Waking Up Saying 'Eh,'" page 98). Your baby will spit out the pacifier if releasing the air requires additional help, and will say "eh" again. At that point, I would suggest trying some of the holds for "eairh" (see chapter 9).

BABY-WEARING IN A SLING

Carrying your baby in a sling is an excellent way to keep him upright while providing warmth and security. Children carried in slings have the constant reassurance of being close to a loved one, and are less likely to be prone to an accumulation of wind as they move around all day while upright. In Bali, slings are little more than a colorful piece of cloth, tied around the front or back and worn by women who need their hands free to tend the fields or manage a handful of other children. There are many excellent commercial models on the market, or you can opt for a handmade sling:

- Fold a large sarong in half.
- Drape it lengthwise over one shoulder.
- Reach around your back and grab the back end and bring it to the front.
- Tie it securely to the other end, at about chest level.
- Place your baby inside the pocket you have created.

taming "the grizzlies": "eh" versus "neh"

HELP FOR THE GRIZZLIES!

If you have children, you know what I mean when I talk about the "grizzly period." Some parents call it the "witching hour." Another friend calls it "arsenic hour." It's that time of the day, usually around 5:00 p.m., when babies are tired and irritable— and so are most parents. As a new mother, I considered this normal, as I'd heard so much about it from friends with children. In fact, when my nieces were babies, I used to drop by to help bathe them to calm them down and give my sister some time to herself.

When I had Toby, he, too, had his grizzly period until I learned about the different cries—especially the difference between "neh" and "eh." I realized his grizzlies were coming from a buildup of wind. For one thing, I hadn't burped him at all unless it was after a feeding. And for another, I thought he was hungry every time he cried. The buildup of wind in his body

*created a very uncomfortable late afternoon for both of us. Once
I started feeding him when he said "neh" and burping him when
he said "eh," the grizzlies gradually disappeared from our lives!*
—FANNY

Exactly when the grizzlies arrive at your house may vary, but with
some babies it seems there's a distinct time of day when they are most
unhappy. Burping your baby more diligently and making sure not to
feed your baby on top of an air bubble can reduce this stressful time.
That's where understanding "eh" and "neh" come to the fore.

Imagine a long, thin cylinder. Now visualize filling three-quarters
of the cylinder with liquid, and an air bubble on top. Now suppose
you start to fill the cylinder again. The air bubble needs to come out
somehow. It does this in one of three ways:

1. sliding out, as a burp
2. coming out as a burp along with the milk atop it
3. traveling down the cylinder, and either accumulating
   with other bubbles that need to come up as burps, or
   moving down to the very bottom and coming out as
   lower-intestinal wind, or gas

The first option from the methods above is the easiest if your baby
has wind, and it can help diminish or prevent the grizzlies. So try
to make sure you burp your baby every time he says "eh," whether
you hear it before a feeding, after a feeding, before a nap, or an hour
after a nap. Listen to your baby and really try to burp him anytime
he cries "eh." I've received many letters from parents saying that the

afternoon crying period is better now that they're burping and feed-ing their babies on demand, according to their cries.

EASY HOLDS FOR "EH" PREVENTION

If you have a windy baby, holding him upright as much as possible can help prevent "eh" from dominating the day. A baby lying in a carriage all afternoon is sure to accumulate wind, and this will be expressed, most loudly, around the early-evening period, just when you might like to have a little time to relax.

If you're really tired or worried about dropping your baby, con-sider these easy ways to keep your baby's body upright: The car-riage could be slanted more to a sitting position. You could carry your baby in a sling while you do chores, prop him on a pillow on the floor while you watch and interact with him, or put him in a bouncy seat. And if you sit down to rest, sit in a comfortable chair and gently cradle him in the crook of your arm, with his bottom resting on your lap.

"eh" versus "neh" and common feeding problems

FEEDING A BABY when what he really needs to do is burp is one of the most common mistakes new parents make. In fact, I would esti-mate that 70 percent of the parents who participated in my language trials did this. If you've done it, too, you are not alone—and you may be surprised at how this single change can help resolve multiple feed-ing problems.

Feeding when your baby is saying "eh" can create problems with breast- and bottle-feeding. Many babies who refuse to attach are actually doing so because they need to burp. When your baby is moving his mouth from side to side over the nipple and not clamping down, try sitting him up and listening to his cry. You may find that he is really saying "eh," not "neh." This doesn't mean that he won't feed; it just means that you need to help him get rid of an air bubble first.

It surprises a lot of people that simply burping their baby before feeding can have a significant impact on how well the baby feeds and for how long. But it makes perfect sense. Think about the last time you drank a big glass of soda. Were you hungry afterward? Generally not, as the gas in the soda has filled your stomach—unless, that is, you've burped it out, in which case you've got room for food. The alternative is that you get hungry an hour or so later, which also happens with your baby. To prevent having to feed your baby every two hours, make sure he has a clear tummy before starting. It can make a world of difference.

"EH" DURING OR IMMEDIATELY AFTER FEEDING

If a baby starts to say "eh" during or right after feeding, you will want to use simple, straightforward burping methods that keep your baby upright to help prevent your baby's spitting up just-consumed milk along with the burp. One of the most common positions is to seat your baby on your lap and gently rub his back. There are variations on this theme (see "Techniques and Tips for Solving 'Eh,'" page 87), and it's simply a matter of trying a few different positions to see which suit you and your baby best. It's a good idea to have several burping techniques at the ready to use at different times, or in combination, depending on what works for your baby.

"EH" BETWEEN FEEDINGS

If your baby says "eh" between feedings during quiet time, often the simple act of picking up your baby will help to move the air out. You'll find that you will instinctively start to pat or rub your baby's back as you walk, and the movement from walking often helps, too. Don't necessarily expect to hear a large burp or even smaller air bubbles; simply the fact that your baby has stopped saying "eh, eh, eh" is a sign that the need has been met. If your baby often says "eh" between feedings, you may need to adjust your baby's lifestyle to a more upright one. Try to hold him more and keep him elevated rather than flat (for tips on sleeping and elevation, see "'Eh' and Your Baby's Sleep," below).

"eh" and your baby's sleep

WE ALL KNOW OF BABIES who fall asleep more easily and sleep better in their car seat. The elevated position, the snug fit, and the movement of the car often make it an ideal place for your baby to get a good nap. While this may be the case, it isn't advisable for your baby to spend long periods of time in his car seat, as it can affect the development of his spine.

If your baby is one that seems happier in the car seat, it's an indicator that you need to burp him more, hold him upright, and adjust his sleeping environment to be more snug and elevated. I have noticed in my studies that the babies who tend to favor sleeping in upright positions tend to be more windy than most, often need a more elevated sleeping environment, and need to be held upright more often. These babies tend to improve dramatically after their parents start to respond to the "eh" sound.

WEARING YOUR "EH" BABY

Wearing your baby instead of putting him down flat has wonderful results for these "eh" babies. The slings that hold the baby upright against your chest are especially effective, as they enable the weight of the baby's own stomach to help move out the air. It's sort of like a continuous burping position, helped by the fact that it's nearly impossible not to rub or gently pat your baby's back when he's snuggled against you in a sling.

CRIB ELEVATION AND THE "EH" BABY

If your baby prefers sleeping upright, elevating his crib can help everyone get more sleep. Do this by elevating the head of his crib or bassinet slightly—but be sure this is done outside the crib rather than on the inside, as we don't want the baby sliding down to the end in a dangerous position.

For the same reason, don't elevate the mattress: make sure the whole crib is elevated at an angle. Elevating just the mattress could result in your baby getting his head caught between the bars and the side of the mattress.

SWADDLING THE "EH" BABY

Babies who suffer from wind often find comfort by being swaddled more firmly around their tummies, with one or both arms free, and with their legs free or loosely wrapped so they can kick and pull them upward. This modified wrap still works to calm the startle reflex that can waken a baby, and the firmness around the tummy can help soothe her, but it also allows movement, to let her wriggle a little more in her efforts to remove wind.

For instructions on swaddling in both the usual and modified ways, see chapter 5.

WAKING UP SAYING "EH"

If your baby wakens crying shortly after falling asleep, he is probably crying "eh." Some parents mistakenly think their baby is hungry or wants to get up. Not so.

The good thing about an air bubble that wakes your baby is that it's generally easy to address. You'll want to solve the problem as quickly as possible, so you can put him back down to finish his nap or continue sleeping. Do this by picking him up and placing him high up over your shoulder, so that his body starts to curve around your shoulder, and pat his back in an upward rhythm. This should quickly get rid of the offending air bubble so you can put him back down to sleep. Be sure to hang on to your baby so he's secure in this position.

This method not only helps ensure that your baby gets enough sleep but also helps create good sleeping habits, so that when he's older and able to move his body to release air bubbles, he will know how to go back to sleep on his own.

MORE BURPING, MORE SLEEPING

It used to be that if August woke crying from a nap, I'd pick him up, change his diaper, and go through all the common settling routines. Often that would be the end of his nap, and he would become increasingly cranky as the day wore on. Now if I hear "eh" in his cry, I know that he only needs a burp and is then happy to go back to sleep. I can't believe how easy it is—one

little burp and he just goes right off again. He's getting so much more sleep, and I've got time to do things around the house.
—FRANCINE

"to chase the wind away"

THIS IS THE LITERAL TRANSLATION of the Thai word for burping. I was fortunate enough to be able to study the parenting style of Thai mothers and the sounds Thai babies made. I loved how even the simplest act of burping a baby was described in almost poetic terms. To me, it symbolized Thai parents' very gentle, hands-on approach to parenting. Instead of burping a baby, a Thai parent "chases the wind away." Listening for "eh" and helping your baby find this kind of comfort may seem mundane, as we do it so often for our babies, but in fact it is a special way of showing your love that your baby very much needs.

PART 2

6-week words

□

Now that you have mastered the three new-born words "neh" ("I'm hungry), "owh" ("I'm tired"), and "eh" ("I need to burp"), you're ready to learn the next set, which your baby may start to make at around six weeks. These sounds will help you meet your baby's needs, once you've addressed the common needs of hunger, wind, and sleep. They give you information about whether your baby has lower-intestinal gas, is too hot or cold, needs to be changed, or has skin irritation.

The six-week words are broken down into two main sounds: "eairh" and "heh." Both have complex subtleties, as sound variations are common and easily identified. However, you will find that "eairh" and "heh" are really all you will need to decode your baby's general needs.

Understanding your baby's cries and responding to what your baby asks for, when he asks for it, is known as parenting "on demand." For newborn babies under twenty weeks of age, this is the best approach. Babies that young are very vulnerable and their bodies are too immature to cope with waiting for a feeding or being kept awake.

Some of the information in these chapters may be familiar to you. But this may be a time when the care of your baby will begin to be shared with a few others you trust, and this information may be helpful to them.

CHAPTER 7

"eairh": "i have gas"

THE SOUND YOUR BABY MAKES when she has intestinal gas is "eairh." Her body will likely be rigid, and she will tend to make sudden, jerky movements, with her chin up.

The reflex that creates the word "eairh" is the tensing of the abdominal muscles of the baby's digestive system. This means that air has become trapped in the digestive system and has moved down into the large intestine. As the baby tries to expel this gas, the muscles of the large intestine contract, which causes cramping and pain.

"Eairh" is similar to the sound that you make when you're straining over a bowel movement. The physical process of passing gas is very similar to that of passing stool and causes a similar feeling of urgency and discomfort. There is a difference in sound, however, as passing gas involves more muscles in the stomach, and the diaphragm moves up when creating the sound.

Intestinal gas in babies has two main causes. The more common cause is air ingested through the nose or mouth, either during feeding or when swallowing excess saliva. Babies who often spit up or who have reflux can have lots of excess saliva. The other cause of intestinal gas is as a by-product of digestion or incomplete digestion. Certain formulas can cause intestinal gas, and so can breast milk, depending on what the breast-feeding mother has eaten.

There are a number of other contributing factors to intestinal gas, including how well the infant latches on to the breast, how fast the flow of milk (breast or bottle) is, or how the bottle is positioned. Gas in the baby's tummy can also result from lack of burping or spending too much time lying flat.

Unfortunately, by the time you hear "eairh," your baby is already upset. As babies can gulp in more air when they are in pain or distress, making the "eairh" worse, don't delay when you hear this sound! Take action immediately, and do all you can to prevent "eairh." While "eairh" can be a word that babies cry for hours on end, if it's dealt with early on, this need can be relieved as easily as hunger or fatigue.

what "eairh" sounds like

TRY TO MAKE THE SOUND yourself: Push your tummy out as far as it will go, and push all the air in your lungs down to your tummy as low as you can. Then, without breathing in, give one last forceful push of air out and you will make an "eeeerrrrrrhhhhhh" sound. The "e" and "r" sounds are produced by the bearing down of the stomach muscles. The "hhh" comes from the expelling of air at the end of the sound. Phonetically we spell it as "eairh."

The more distressed your baby becomes, the more it actually sounds as though he is saying "air," with a distinct "r r r" at the end. You also can hear the sound "eairh" in words like "errand," "errant," and "bear."

how "eairh" is made

WHEN YOU LOOK at your baby's face, you will notice that her mouth is half open, her tongue is back, and there is obvious distress on her face. You may also notice that your baby's stomach is hardened and that her body is more rigid than usual.

hearing "eairh"

THIS SOUND CAN BECOME fast and furious. You need to observe the velocity of the cry, the length of each phonetic sound, and other physically easy-to-see signs to determine what action to take. If the baby produces the sound "eairh" easily and the sound is clear, without other crying sounds, she probably has just normal gas. Her tummy will still be malleable and softish to touch, her head will be in a normal position, and she will be leaving space between each word cried. All of this adds up to generalized discomfort that you can relieve using the holds in chapter 9.

If the cry is more elongated, as in "eeeeerrrrrrrrrrrrhhhh," with more "r" sound, then you may notice that your baby's tummy is becoming hard, that she is starting to lift her chin, and her mouth is wide and open, with her tongue back. The cry is forceful and loud, and makes many parents feel physically uncomfortable. When this happens, it's important to realize that this sound will take some time to resolve.

"Eairh" is one of the most difficult words for parents to deal with, mostly because it is time-consuming to help a baby who is cramping with gas. A baby who is saying "neh" can be fed. A baby who is saying "owh" can be put to bed. A baby who is saying "eh" can be burped. But a baby who is saying "eairh" needs to be calmed down and massaged until the gas is worked out of her system and the cramping dies away, and this can take some time. Your baby will not necessarily stop crying quickly, so it can be very frustrating and upsetting for you, especially if it's the middle of the night and you are sleep deprived. As long as you are hearing the "eairh" sound, though, you can be sure you are doing the right thing by helping your baby to move the air out of her system.

CHAPTER 8

"heh" (and variations): "i'm uncomfortable"

U NCOMFORTABLE" ENCOMPASSES a large array of grievances for a baby, but this word specifically relates to reflexes surrounding the skin. Because the skin is our largest organ and works in synergy with many different muscles, we find that when listening to a baby's cry, we hear similar sounds for issues linked to skin reflexes.

When we get cold, we get goose bumps and shiver; when we get hot, we start to perspire; when we have irritation our skin swells and gets red in a process that protects our bodies from bacteria. All this happens for babies, too. And all these responses come under "heh."

These reflexes are accompanied by other body reflexes, like increased heart rate, opening the limbs to cool down, or curling up to get warm. This physical coordination of our muscles happens in sequence, depending on what the skin is regulating, and it is this sequence that affects the sound your baby makes. "Heh" is the word for "uncomfortable," but it stands to reason that needing one's diaper changed is different from feeling hot or cold. Although there are differences in the sound to indicate when your baby is hot, cold, has skin irritation, or needs a different position, they are all governed by the one main organ, which is the skin.

"Heh" and its variants are generally solved in similar ways, so categorizing them all under one word is simplest and makes the life of a new parent easier. I'll explain the slight differences in sound, but I have found that parents do quite well knowing only "heh."

what "heh" sounds like

"HEH" IS A BREATHY SOUND, like a sigh but with more force—like an expulsion of air with pressure. You can hear the sound "heh" at the beginning of words such as "hectic," "help," "hindrance," and "heffalump."

To make this sound yourself, relax your body and take a deep breath. Place the tip of your tongue against the base of your bottom teeth, open your mouth in a wide fake smile and breathe out quickly. Now try it again, adding voice to it, and you'll hear a "heh" sound.

You will also feel that the sound comes from a heady place away from the nasal cavity, more toward the back of the throat. Take a moment to explore this by saying "eairh," which involves using your lower abdomen; then say "neh," which brings the sound toward the nasal cavity; then follow it now with the "heh" sound. You can feel that these sounds come from and affect different parts of your body.

how "heh" is made

WHEN WE GET HOT, our heart pumps our blood harder, our veins expand, and we spread our limbs wider: legs apart, arms out. When we get cold, the blood vessels in our extremities constrict, keeping the blood flow closer to our vital organs. We bring our limbs close to our bodies to help keep us warm. These changes also affect our breath. When we are hot, our exhalation is more prominent; when we are cold, our inhalation is slower and more noticeable. And when some part of our body itches, we squirm and move to try to reach the place so we can rub it.

All of these physical, muscular changes help to shape the sound that you will hear in your baby's cry when she feels these discomforts.

hearing "heh"

THE SPECIFIC DISCOMFORT your baby feels will affect the sound she makes, based on the rate of airflow over her larynx or the movement of her mouth and tongue. Nonetheless, what you are listening for essentially is the "h" at the front of the sound that tells you that your baby is uncomfortable. The nuances following the "h" sound are simply added details that give you an insight into how she is uncomfortable.

"HEH" VARIATION—"HORH": "I'M COLD."
When you hear a long "heh" that changes to finish with an "orrh," your baby is getting cold. You will notice that he will bring his limbs

in close to his body and that the sound is cried relatively calmly. His tongue moves up from his bottom gum to the top, almost trapping the air, effectively warming it before it goes down to the lungs. As a result, we hear a "horh" sound.

"HEH" VARIATION—"HEHEHEH": "I'M HOT."

The opposite physical reaction occurs with heat, where the sound starts as "heh" but changes into a short, quick, repetitious "heheheh." Here the tongue flattens even more and air is taken in quickly and released quickly, almost like a pant. Sound is heard on the inhalation as well as on the exhalation, producing "heheheheh." If you copy this sound, you can feel the cooling effects of the air.

"HEH" VARIATION—"HEIR": "I ITCH [OR HAVE OTHER SURFACE DISCOMFORT]."

When a baby has an itch or surface discomfort, such as a rash, he will tend to squirm and grimace, with brow furrowed. The squirming produces an irregular output of air; the grimace, a sound like "ei." You'll hear an "heir" sound, rarely said singularly, but usually within a "sentence" of baby sounds. To make this sound yourself, breathe in, and as you breathe out move your shoulders quickly one at a time, up and down. Grimace and pull your mouth wide, tongue at the base of your bottom teeth.

"HEH" AS THE MAIN SOUND

When our baby needs a change of position, a clear and easy "heh" is produced by a solid expelling of air. In all the other instances, it is the back part of this sound that changes, depending on the discomfort, but they all start with "heh." This is why simply listening for the "heh" or "h" sound within your baby's cry is really all you need. When you hear it, you'll know that your baby is uncomfortable, and you can try responding to different comfort needs. If you're able, listen for the back part of the sound to get the details, but most parents find that just knowing "heh" is more than enough.

CHAPTER 9

"eairh" solutions

THE RELIEF OF FINALLY UNDERSTANDING

I should have realized that my daughter would be a gassy sort of person, because I am! But I could never understand what was going on with her. She started out sleeping and feeding well, but at about five weeks, things started going downhill. She was cranky all the time, and slept hardly at all, and acted as if she wanted to feed—but then she wouldn't. She wasn't curled up in a ball or making fists the way babies with gas are supposed to do. When I heard and understood my little girl saying "eairh" one day, I got tingles down my spine. It was a moment of realization: finally I knew what was upsetting her. –CATHERINE

"Eairh" is the word you will hear in your baby's cry when she has gas. The sound is made by the muscles acting in a cramp-like motion in an effort to expel air out of your baby's bottom. You will notice that often your baby's stomach will be distended and hard when you hear this sound and that her body is stiff. As soon as the gas has been expelled or even moved, you will notice that your baby's body relaxes and she stops crying. "Eairh" is usually heard at the end of the day during the period of afternoon fussiness many babies experience, caused by an accumulation of air from the day's events. Other causes are colic, lactose intolerance, allergy to certain foods, or just general inactivity.

Responding quickly is particularly important, as by the time you hear "eairh," your baby is probably already upset. Fortunately, there are many solutions to try.

In one of the early language trials I conducted, I saw all the participants in the space of one weekend. Forty mothers and forty crying babies, all day long, for the entire weekend. It was quite a challenge! The lasting impression of that weekend, however, was the similarity of problems mothers were experiencing. Most of the babies were having trouble with wind and gas, and very few mothers could detect it. Until their baby was screaming and demonstrating signs of being in abdominal pain—drawing his legs up and clenching his fists—most mothers did not think of gas as being an issue for their babies. Then, once they had dealt with the problem, they did not consider the issue of gas again. But wind and gas can happen anytime—and can keep on happening—so observe your baby and listen for "eairh."

the over-the-shoulder hold

THIS HOLD is very effective for "eairh."

- While standing, place your baby up high over your shoulder so that his lower body is positioned over your shoulder blade. Make sure you hold him very securely.
- Maintaining your secure hold, rotate your shoulder so that it is gently massaging your baby's stomach. The weight of your baby's body, coupled with the movement from your shoulder, will help move the air out. You will notice that your baby will be quite stiff when you start, and then become curved

around the top of your shoulder as the pain subsides. As it does so, you will often hear your baby make groaning sounds of pleasure, especially if you rub or pat his lower back.

- If your baby is very upset, you can walk or pace as you do this hold, as the rhythmic movement can be soothing. If you find that your arms become tired, lift the baby up higher so that the weight is being taken by your shoulder, or alternate with another hold.

the football hold

THIS HOLD is a good one for dads, as their forearms tend to be large and strong.

- Position your baby so he straddles your forearm, stomach down, with his head facing the crook of your elbow and his legs across your hand. You can use your hand to hook around your baby's legs, holding him securely. The weight from his body will push his stomach into your arm. The warmth from your arm will help to soothe a sore stomach.
- You can use your other hand to rub or pat your baby's back, or to support your other arm underneath. A variation of this hold includes doing the hold while walking around, as this movement can help push your arm into the baby's stomach, and the rhythm of walking can be soothing. Another variation is reversing the baby's position so he is still facedown, but his head and upper chest are cradled in your hand.

"bicycling"

PLACING YOUR BABY on his back on your lap, gently move his legs as if he were pedaling a bicycle. This pumping action helps to stretch out his tummy muscles and move his "innards" so that the air bubble moves into a different and more comfortable place.

baby yoga poses

YOU WILL NOTICE that when your baby is crying "eairh," she tends to curl her legs toward her tummy.

- Place your baby on your lap, on her back, facing you.
- Placing one hand on her tummy, with your other hand gently move her right leg into a straight position, hold for a few seconds, and then gently move it up onto her stomach with her knee bent. Repeat three times, then switch legs.
- Remove your hand from her stomach and do the same movement with both legs together.

the over-the-knee hold

I LIKE THIS HOLD the best, because it enables the parent to switch off, especially if feeling stressed by her crying baby. I think people underestimate how stressful having a crying baby can be—particularly when it's late at night and you have accumulated a sleep

115

deficit. Having a hold like this in such times can be a godsend to parents. This hold lets you watch TV or read a book while still helping to solve the problem your baby is having. Even if you have a baby who doesn't cry a lot, this is a soothing method that is quick and easy. However, it is *not* a hold to do on a full stomach, after a feeding.

- Start in a comfortable position, cross your leg over your knee, and place your baby facedown so that his stomach curls over your top leg. You will find that he will be quite stiff when you first place him in this position.
- Rock your legs from side to side to create a slow, rocking motion, holding your baby in place with your hand on his lower back. The rhythm is very soothing for both baby and parent! You can either rub his back or simply let the heat from your hand soothe him.
- If he is very upset, you can also gently roll him over your leg, in small movements back and forth.

tummy time

- Roll up a hand towel lengthwise, lay it on a flat surface, and place your baby facedown on top, with her stomach over the towel. In a fanlike forward motion, rub her lower back in rotation with your thumbs. Sometimes a small amount of baby oil can reduce friction and make the motion smoother. The oil also helps to hold the baby's body heat against the lower-back area.

- Never leave your baby alone in this position, and certainly never be tempted to let her sleep this way—even if it is the only position in which she is calm.

warm water

IF YOUR BABY is too upset to massage and is not upset by being placed in water (some babies are), a warm bath is an ideal way to soothe and gently distract a baby who is saying "eairh." Cradle your baby in the water in one arm and use the other hand to massage his tummy so that you are providing a strong sense of security while working on the area of pain.

My son didn't like baths, but he did like being in the shower, and during his bad moments a quick shower would often do the trick. It was probably a combination of the sound, the steam, and being held that helped. Obviously because babies' skin is so fragile and can burn easily, I turned the hot water down to barely warm, so as not to scald my baby. It was a little unpleasant for me, but it was worthwhile, as he would stop crying. I was then able to massage his tummy, and on the bad nights have him fall asleep in the over-the-knee hold.

massage

MASSAGE IS one of the best ways to calm an irritable baby, unless his skin is particularly sensitive. In many countries, massage is a daily part of caring for a baby. Massage is beneficial not only because of the soothing physical contact; it has also been shown to have some effect on a baby's immune system, circulation, and digestion. There are no special skills required—just plenty of patience!

Some babies do not like being dressed and then undressed, so if your goal is to soothe an anxious or screaming baby, it might be best to leave him as he is, dressed or undressed. If you are going to massage your baby dressed or if you don't have any oil, it's okay. You can still perform the motions to great effect without using oil.

- First, prepare the environment. Find a warm, soothing spot. Make sure the room has no drafts, because your baby's core temperature drops quickly, particularly if he is undressed. If you're using oil, place a waterproof cloth under a soft, non-irritating blanket or towel and lay your baby on his back. Although using oil ensures that your strokes are smooth and gentle, your baby is likely to pick up the oil on his fingers and put them in his mouth, so choose a plant-based oil such as grape seed or sweet almond. Manufactured baby oils contain petroleum extracts.

- Place your hand under your baby's chin with your fingers facing out. Gently stroke down your baby's chest until your palm is over his belly button. Once there, pull your hand gently across his tummy to his side. Repeat the process using the other hand, moving across to the alternate side once your hand has reached his belly button. Once you are confident of the movement—and if your baby isn't the wriggly kind—you can use both hands, with one following the other.

- Next, slowly push your baby's legs up toward his tummy. Hold them there for a few seconds; then bring his legs back down and repeat the action.
- Repeat the whole process until your baby feels better.
- Long strokes are calming. Also, go with the baby's movements. Babies tend to wriggle, pull their legs up, move side to side, and so on. If your baby is doing that, don't try to force his legs down straight so you can stroke all the way down. Just move your hands in a gentle, flowing, swirling motion down his body and back up again. If he turns to the side as you do so, stroke down or up his side. Unlike a more systematic massage for adults, this is really about touch and encompassing the baby in your hands, soothing his digestion while gently stimulating his skin and muscles.

SOOTHING "EAIRH" CAN BE SOOTHING FOR YOU, TOO

When I got home from work one evening, I found my daughter Lorna in obvious discomfort, crying the "eairh" word. I immediately put her high up on my shoulder and used the rotation technique [see chapter 6]. I asked the babysitter to run a warm bath while I began to massage Lorna's tummy and back. Then I finished by giving her a warm, relaxing bath. I found this routine worked well to settle her in the evenings when things were getting a little unsettled—and it settled me, too. It was so helpful to come home from work and be able to slot in this special time of caring for my baby. I could just listen to her and know what to do! —MADINE

pacifiers and "eairh"

IF YOUR BABY GETS COMFORT from a pacifier, use one! At the same time, continue to focus on doing the "eairh" solutions. You may find that when you give a pacifier to a baby crying "eairh," she will suck hard for a few moments, then spit it out. I would advise using a pacifier at the end of an "eairh" episode. With the new research that links pacifiers to helping prevent SIDS and the tiredness that often comes from having an uncomfortable tummy, any extra comfort and stress relief is a good thing. Always put the baby to bed on her back, and preferably close by, if it has been a particularly difficult period.

to wrap, or not to wrap?

YOU MAY HAVE BEEN TOLD that babies need to be tightly swaddled when they go to sleep. As you learned when reading about "owh," babies can often work wind and gas out of their systems as they move around in their sleep. They cannot do this if they are tightly bound. I found the best way to help Tomas move wind was to wrap his tummy tightly but leave the blanket a little loose around his legs and arms. That way he could shift some of the gas himself. Meanwhile, the wrap around his tummy helped ease the pain. Babies differ in their preferences, so experiment with wrapping a few different ways and see how your baby responds.

head it off before it starts: "eairh" prevention strategies

IT'S SAID THAT an ounce of prevention is worth a pound of cure. Here are some things you can to do to help prevent or minimize "eairh."

CARRYING, BURPING, AND WATCHING FOR PATTERNS

Carry your baby as much as possible throughout the day, preferably in a sling. The body contact will provide security for a sensitive baby, and the vertical position will help resolve wind problems. There is no possible negative outcome of doing this; you cannot "spoil" a baby under the age of five months.

Be sure to burp your baby throughout the day. Certainly make sure that you burp her whenever you hear the sound "eh." The aim is to get the air bubbles out before they go down through the digestive system. An "eh" earlier can become "eairh" later, and may be harder to manage.

Keep your baby upright as much as possible. Do this by holding the baby against you rather than cradling her across you.

If there is a pattern to your baby's saying "eairh"—for example, if she tends to have a period of unsettled "eairhs" around 6:00 p.m. (the typical time for what's often called the "witching hour" or the "grizzlies")—work in harmony with her pattern. Add a calming technique, such as a warm bath or a massage, before the grizzlies hit. It can make all the difference. It relaxes both baby and parent, and if there are crying bouts, it often makes them shorter and less forceful.

121

MOTHER'S DIET

When you are nursing, what you eat affects your baby. My son was only a few weeks old when I discovered that he suffered from allergies, as well as colic and reflux. As I had been ill and was looking after my baby on my own, I had been living on smoothies and yogurt, as they were easy to make and easy to eat. There were a couple of days when I had run out of milk and couldn't get to the store. I noticed a subtle shift in Tomas. The "eairh" word was not so prevalent, and it occurred to me that he might have a dairy intolerance. For the next few weeks I experimented with dropping certain foods and drinks from my diet. Without fail, every time I drank milk, Tomas suffered. I was very, very careful after that about my milk intake. After a year of breast-feeding a lactose-intolerant child, I will never forget the taste of rice milk!

If your baby is frequently saying "eairh," consider your diet. Allergies are not the only issue—there are certain foods, such as garlic, cabbage, broccoli, foods sweetened with fructose, and dairy products, that create more air as they are digested than other foods. This is why doctors often advocate a simple diet with as few processed foods as possible for nursing mothers. Your pediatrician can give you a list of "suspect" foods. If you are going to eat any of these foods, be aware of the reaction your baby might have, and be prepared to spend time managing the problem.

SPICE: NOT ALWAYS NICE

I was so excited to be back at work that when the time came for lunch, I joined my colleagues at an Indian restaurant. I enjoyed the delicious spicy dishes along with everyone else, not even thinking that it might affect my breast milk! The next day, Annabel was definitely saying "eairh"! I realized it was probably caused by her early introduction to Indian cuisine. Instead of trying to rock her to sleep or put her in front of a mobile to amuse her, I knew immediately that I should pick her up and hold her upright. I popped her up on my shoulder and walked around the house for a while, switching to the over-the-knee method when I got tired. Dealing with a problem is always much easier when you know what the problem is and that you can do something to prevent it. —DEB

If you're breast-feeding, it's important that you have good nutrition and that you have enough calories to be able to produce your best possible milk. Try to keep to unseasoned or plain foods and dishes as much as possible, and then slowly add in other, more complex meals. Keep a diary of what you ate and when, and note the time when your baby was unsettled (saying "eairh" or being fussy, whiny, or just not herself—you'll know your baby's language well enough by now to know that she wasn't making the sounds for hunger, tiredness, or needing to burp), as these might correlate to things you ate. Remember, you will need to allow time for your body's digestion and conversion of nutrition into breast milk, and then your baby's digestion of your breast milk, before you can connect a food to a possible reaction.

To get started, here are some general guidelines.

- Foods like fruits and berries, if they cause a reaction at all, tend to manifest as rashes on the baby. So, if your baby gets diaper rash the day after you have consumed a pint of strawberries, consider eliminating the berries. (The word your baby will say if her skin is uncomfortable is "heir"—see chapter 8.)

- Products that contain flavorings (such as MSG) tend to produce headaches, causing the baby to make a sound similar to the teething sound, "gen," mixed with "heh." This can occur anywhere up to three days after your consumption.
- Tomatoes can produce either rashes or headaches.
- Dairy can produce the "eairh" word and colic-type symptoms that come on suddenly. You will also notice that the baby will spit up more if there is a dairy sensitivity.
- Cabbage, beans, broccoli, Brussels sprouts, and lentils are some examples of foods you may consume that produce gas in your baby—but techniques such as burping and keeping the baby upright can counteract them.
- Products containing wheat, rye, barley, oats, corn, and other grasses can produce discomfort and redness around the baby's joints; she will say "heir" (see chapter 8) more regularly.
- Aged cheese and chocolate can cause headache and upset stomach.

change formulas

IF YOUR BABY IS CONTINUING long bouts of crying "eairh" day after day, perhaps she has a problem with the formula. Some babies have trouble digesting lactose and may need a special formula, as discussed in chapter 4.

Consult your heath professional about changing formulas, as you might need a specialty formula such as:

- *Lactose-free, cow's-milk-based formulas.* These are similar to the usual cow's-milk-based formula but contain no lactose. They're used when a baby presents as lactose intolerant.
- *Soybean-based formulas.* These are based on soy protein extracts. Fat from vegetable oils, and carbohydrates from cornstarch and sucrose are added, as are iron, vitamins, and minerals. This formula is used if your baby is truly allergic to cow's milk.
- *Goat's-milk-based formula.* Goat's-milk-based formula is new to being recognized as safe for newborn babies. It is an alternative for babies who are allergic to both cow's- milk-based and soy-based formulas.
- *Extensively hydrolyzed formula.* This type of formula is aimed at helping to prevent allergies in babies when there is a family history of allergies such as asthma, hay fever, eczema, or nut or soy allergies.

Even if you keep the same type of formula but change brands, keep an ear on your baby's cries to see if the change is agreeing with her. I remember working with one mother whose baby reacted strongly to changing to a cheaper brand of formula, crying for as long as three hours within half an hour of feeding. Once the baby had her old formula back, the crying episodes stopped.

"eairh" and colic

I HAVE OBSERVED that colicky babies often produce "eairh" in their cries. This does not mean that if your baby says "eairh" he has colic.

The word "colic" is used to describe a situation in which a baby—usually between the ages of two weeks and six months—has extensive daily crying episodes that are very difficult to calm, and often for which there is no obvious reason. Colic is usually diagnosed by your pediatrician, who will be able to make sure nothing more serious is wrong, as well as offer solutions for resolving the issue.

Responding to your baby's cries and satisfying your baby's needs as they occur throughout the day can really help to reduce colic episodes. Feeding as soon as a baby says "neh" improves the baby's feed, reducing air being sucked in during feeding. Regardless of the diagnosis, understanding and acting on "eairh" will help reduce gas, as will burping your baby when he says "eh." The aim with this "prevention before cure" thinking is that we want to stop the wind before it causes our baby to be curled up and screaming.

"Gas" and "colic" are often used to mean the same thing, but this is not necessarily true. Colic is often associated with digestive issues, because many babies seem to suffer from a bloated stomach during a colic episode. Resolution of digestive issues—relating either to feeding or burping—and the maturing of the digestive system seem to resolve the colicky episodes.

It is often suggested that crying itself contributes to the colicky bloating by increasing the amount of air the baby swallows. If your baby suffers from colic and says "eairh," treat him for lower wind first. If your baby still does not settle, there may be other causes that become apparent. Be patient and don't give up. Expect resolving colic to take some time—there aren't immediate fixes; it's really a process of resolution.

"upright parenting" and "parenting right"

OFTEN WHAT WE ARE TAUGHT as new parents can be exactly the opposite of what is required when a baby is suffering from gas. We burp our babies only after feedings, not before, which means we may be feeding them when their tummies are filled with air bubbles. The trapped air gets pushed from the upper digestive system to the lower part of the system—and then we are trying to get our baby to sleep when he has a tummy full of gas.

If you take a different view of the "right" way to burp your baby and help him to clear the wind from his upper digestive system regularly, you will not hear "eairh" much at all. If you are hearing "eairh" often, you have a particularly windy baby. It is a good idea to burp him and massage his lower digestive region often—even when he's not saying "eairh." Adopt an "upright parenting" philosophy of keeping your baby vertical as much as possible, even in sleep (for tips on how to safely raise the head of the crib, see chapter 6). And remember, by the time you are hearing "eairh," you have missed prevention and need to look for the cure. Above all, especially if your baby is colicky, try to keep in mind that your baby is operating by unconscious reflex. He cannot help what he is doing. By using your baby's language to understand his needs, you are doing the very best you can for him.

CHAPTER 10

"heh" solutions

HEARING "HEH" GETS EASIER

"Heh" was a sound I found a little difficult to hear at first, but once I understood that the "h" represented the sound of breath moving out, it became much easier. I just thought of a dog's pant, and added more sound or vocalization to it: "heh, heh, heh." I also noticed that the variations of the sound—"horh" for cold, or "heir" for skin irritation—were easy to hear. Not only are the phonetics slightly different, but also the way my baby says them is different. I found "heh" the most useful word of the baby-language words—aside from "neh," of course! —TARA

"Heh" is the word for "uncomfortable." This sound is governed by the organ of the skin and the reflexes it stimulates in the baby's muscles and organs. It could mean your baby needs a diaper change, is bothered by diaper rash, is too hot or cold, or simply wants her physical position to be changed. Although there are other sounds associated with skin irritation that give us more information, you really need to know only "heh." Usually, just knowing that your baby has an uncomfortable feeling relating to her skin is enough to help you sort through the different comfort needs until you can resolve your baby's issue.

diaper changing and "heh"

BABIES WILL TEND to want to have their diaper changed when it becomes uncomfortable. This could be because it has become too heavy or has moved into an uncomfortable place, the wetness is making the baby cold, or her skin is getting irritated. In order to prevent diaper rash, it's a good idea to change your baby as often as possible and to make sure the diaper fits correctly.

cloth versus disposable

THIS IS A CONTENTIOUS ISSUE for some. Parenting can often bring out very strong feelings in regard to things like breast-feeding, diapers, and immunizations. I think it is always good to look at both sides, be aware of your own lifestyle, and decide what best suits your family. Some families prefer cloth diapers; some like disposable; others use a mixture of both. I personally used a mixture, especially when I took Tom with me on research trips.

CLOTH DIAPERS

These days, cloth diapers no longer mean folding a towel-like square into a triangle and pinning it in place with large safety pins. Modern cloth diapers come in different sizes for a perfect fit, have leak guards around the legs, and fasten with Velcro instead of pins. If Velcro doesn't suit, you can buy Y-snaps that pin the diaper in place without the need for sharp objects.

There are also flushable diaper liners, or you can use washable ones and simply scrape the feces into the toilet before soaking the liner. There are many tools that help with this process, including a special showerhead or rubber scrapers. But my personal opinion is that, since the bathroom is usually a high-traffic area, it's best to keep the area as uncluttered as possible, especially if you have other little children.

The great thing about cloth diapers is that they enable you to control the detergents that are close to your baby's skin, and for babies who say "heir" regularly, this is important.

DISPOSABLE DIAPERS

Disposable diapers are more convenient, as you simply use them and throw them out. Disposable diapers are good for babies who suffer from diaper rash, as they can help keep them dryer for longer. They are, however, more expensive than cloth diapers. My experience is that you may need to try out a few to find the one that works best for your budget and for your baby. My son had an allergy to the glue used in the waistbands of most disposable diapers. There was only one brand that didn't give him a reaction, so when we traveled overseas I had to make sure I brought a suitcase full. Even the same brand, manufactured differently in another country, would irritate him.

Disposable diapers come in different sizes and are designed for different stages, starting with newborn and moving up to pull-up and training pants. Pick the right size for your baby, one that is comfortable but not too tight around the legs or tummy.

Make sure to have a good supply handy, as your baby will use at least ten a day, but also be aware that babies grow at an astounding rate.

WITH "HEH," EVERYONE RESTS EASIER

I woke one morning around 3:00 a.m. to cries of "heh" coming from baby James's crib, so I reached over and felt him, hoping to gently rock him back to sleep. Checking his diaper, though, I found it to be saturated, along with the bedclothes, the mattress, and all his clothing. Even his toy rabbit hadn't escaped a drenching! It turned out the diaper had been fastened too loosely, resulting in a wet bed. Had I ignored his sounds, James would have woken fully before long and both of us would have had our sleep disturbed. By dealing with the situation then, I was able to make James comfortable, letting him drift back into a sound sleep—and returned to bed for a good four hours of undisturbed rest. —ROSALIE

how to change a diaper

I INCLUDE THIS SECTION, although it may seem self-evident, because incorrectly fastening a diaper or not changing it often enough are two of the main reasons we hear "heh." A simple mistake like not folding down a little boy's penis when the diaper is put on can lead to clothes and bedding getting wet. This brings on the inevitable "horh" variation, indicating being cold. Likewise, a babysitter who is nervous about changing a diaper may be inclined to leave it on longer than is best, and then wonder why the baby is crying "heir." Even a small amount of urine can hurt an already sore bottom.

GET PREPARED

- Change the diaper in a warm, dry, safe area. If you choose a changing table, make sure it has anti-roll sides to it, and always keep your hand on your baby to prevent him from falling off. The same goes for any elevated surface, be it a bed, a couch, or a stroller.
- Use a mat or cover to protect the furniture, preferably something with a fabric top that is soft against your baby's skin but has a plastic backing to prevent leakage. Make sure it is easy to wash, and have a spare for when one is in the wash.
- Have all your supplies ready and handy. A newborn baby can go through as many as ten diapers a day, so make sure you have a good supply. If you're using cloth diapers, you will need a cover and pins or diaper fasteners. Keep a diaper pail ready for cloth diapers, or bags for disposable diapers. Have wipes or water and cotton balls for cleaning, and some ointment, powder, or petroleum jelly available for diaper rash.
- If at first you are a little uncomfortable, be assured that you will have lots of chances to practice, and in no time you will be an expert. It won't be long before you'll be able to use diaper-changing time as a fun interaction with your new baby.

CHANGING YOUR BABY

- Place your baby on his back on top of your changing mat and open or remove his clothing.
- Loosen the diaper, and with the front half, wipe away any feces into the middle of the diaper.

- Gently lift your baby's bottom by holding his legs with one hand, and use the back half of the diaper to wipe the feces from his bottom into the middle of the diaper. Remove the dirty diaper from underneath your baby's bottom by folding it in on itself and sliding it out.
- Use baby wipes, a wet cloth, or wet cotton balls to clean the feces or urine from your baby's bottom, remembering to clean in the folds of your baby's skin. Do your best not to pull his skin, but rather clean using small lifting motions. Start at the front and move to the back, lifting his bottom again by holding his legs or ankles. It is especially important to make sure you wipe front to back if you have a girl, from her vagina to her bottom, as this helps to prevent bacteria from the anal area entering the vagina or the urethra and causing an infection.
- Do your best to pat dry or air dry for a few moments; then apply ointment or powder if needed.
- Open up the new diaper, and place it opened up next to your baby. Lift your baby's bottom, again by holding the legs, slide the clean diaper under your baby's bottom, and lower your baby down into the diaper. It should be positioned with the back half under his lower back and bottom, so the front can be lifted between his legs.
- Try to avoid bunching around the legs by making sure the waistband is spread wide and flat. If you have a boy, remember to make sure his penis is facing downward and not upward; otherwise your baby will have a wet tummy—and maybe wet clothes and bedclothes, too.

- Fasten the diaper securely, making sure that it isn't gaping around the legs, or too tight or too loose around the tummy. If you have a newborn, be sure not to cover the umbilical cord. This may mean that you have to fold down the front waistband for a couple of weeks.
- Dress your baby and put him in a safe place while you dispose of the dirty diaper and wash your hands.
- As your baby gets older, you may find that he wriggles and becomes difficult to hold still during a diaper change. Remember, safety first, so if necessary, change him on a mat on the floor.
- Keep a few toys to distract your baby while you change him, such as interesting rattles, or a hanging mobile or mirror above the changing table; or sing and play rhymes such as "The Itsy Bitsy Spider."

"heh" and car seats, bouncy chairs, beds, and mats

YOU'D BE SURPRISED how uncomfortable being in one position can be, and we often don't realize how often we adjust our own bodies to be more comfortable. Our babies can't yet make these adjustments, so they rely on us to do it for them, moving their bodies into comfortable positions. If a baby finds herself sinking down in her stroller, she can ask you to assist only by crying. She doesn't know exactly what is happening, but she knows her body feels uncomfortable. The same happens if she's in a car seat and the straps are too tight. She doesn't have an understanding of what straps are, but she will know that something is pushing her body, making it feel constricted. At times like these, babies will say "heh."

When you hear this sound, check to see if you need to change your baby's position, adjust her clothing, or simply exercise her body. You may find that the diaper was put on too tightly, that the wetness is making her skin feel uncomfortable (this is different from discomfort from a rash or irritation), or that she prefers one arm out when swaddled.

Going anywhere outside the house with a new baby can be a major feat. By the time you feed him, burp him, change him twice because he spit up on the first outfit, pack the day bag, then quickly dress yourself, you can be utterly exhausted. One mother I worked with was rushing to get to an appointment when she strapped her daughter into her stroller. It wasn't long before her daughter started crying. Hearing "heh," the mother checked and saw the problem immediately: she had done up the stroller straps the wrong way and they were digging into her daughter. Usually when you hear "heh," it's a simple problem that needs fixing.

when "heh" becomes "heir"

"HEIR" MEANS that your baby's skin is irritated. It can take the form of rashes, inflamed skin, and itching. Such skin conditions, anywhere, are frustrating and uncomfortable. Even adults wriggle and try to reach the burning or itching area. Our babies do the same thing, and when they are uncomfortable, their "heh" changes to include a sound like "r," as in "heir."

The most common form of skin irritation is diaper rash, but

babies can get rashes in all sorts of places—especially at their joints and also in the folds of their skin.

DIAPER RASH

Diaper rash is red, puffy, and tender-looking skin that appears in the region under the diaper. It can come and go and can have many causes, but the most common cause is infrequently changed diapers. Teething can cause diarrhea, which can in turn cause or exacerbate diaper rash. Breast-feeding mothers may find that when they eat certain foods, usually things like strawberries, peaches, or even tomatoes, these items can cause a reaction in their babies (an allergic reaction in the baby giving rise to a rash, chemical changes in the baby's urine or feces that irritate the baby's skin, or both). Medications such as antibiotics have also been linked to sore bottoms of little ones. When you start your baby on solids, this can cause acidic urine and create the perfect environment for diaper rash.

Diaper rash is uncomfortable and can make your baby unhappy. Addressing "heir" in this instance could be as simple as changing her diaper, or you may need to apply a topical cream as well. Once the rash has appeared, you may find that your baby's bottom becomes even more sensitive and you may need to use hypoallergenic products, or products containing no fragrance or preservative. Consider switching to a pH-controlled bath soap, try to use water and cotton balls instead of commercial wipes, and let your baby's bottom dry in the open air as much as possible. Change diapers often, as urine can sting an already sore bottom.

One father I know noticed that his son, who had been troubled by diaper rash, was crying "heir" a lot more. Because the father was checking the diaper and rash situation frequently, he noticed that his son said "heir" just after wetting the diaper. He concluded that the urine must be stinging the rash. He wiped on a sheer, protective layer of Vaseline after diaper changes. Problem solved.

IRRITATION FROM STOOL AND URINE

Prolonged exposure to urine or feces can irritate a baby's sensitive skin. Your baby may be more prone to diaper rash if she is experiencing frequent bowel movements, because feces are more irritating than urine.

INTRODUCTION OF NEW FOODS

As babies start to eat solid foods, generally between four and twelve months, the content of their stool changes, increasing the likelihood of diaper rash. Changes in your baby's diet can also increase the frequency of stools, which can lead to diaper rash. If you're breast-feeding, your baby may develop diaper rash in response to something you've eaten, such as tomato-based foods. I worked with one mother who discovered that her eating spicy food made her baby say "heir." When your baby starts to eat solid foods, it is important to introduce foods one at a time and to start with low-allergy choices such as rice, pears, potato, and sweet potato, to name some. If you're not sure what foods are low allergy, consult your pediatrician.

IRRITATION FROM A NEW PRODUCT

Babies' skin is very sensitive, and everyday things like detergents, fabric softeners, disposable wipes, or even a new brand of disposable diaper can all cause irritation. For some babies, even baby lotion and oils can cause a problem. If you have a baby like this, you will find that you may need to double rinse your baby's clothing and experiment with different brands of detergents, diapers, and wipes. Some parents find success by wiping the baby's bottom with a low-allergy wipe to remove bacteria, feces, and urine, and following it with a cotton ball soaked in water to remove any residue from the wipe. Pat dry and leave the bottom to air dry for a few minutes. You will probably find that a baby who is sensitive to diaper rash will also have skin irritation on other areas of her body, such as under her arms or behind her knees.

BACTERIAL OR YEAST (FUNGAL) INFECTION

Sometimes what can begin as diaper rash may turn into an infection that can spread to the surrounding region. The diaper can create a perfect environment for the breeding of bacteria and yeast, because the diaper keeps the area warm and moist. Infections can also start in the folds of your baby's skin and in the skin around her joints. These rashes tend to start in the creases of the skin, and once there, they are hard to dry and keep clean without pulling at the skin. A good trick is to use a simple hand fan after patting dry your baby's bottom, underarms, and other places. This is very helpful when you don't have time for air drying. Make sure you have washed the area thoroughly, even in the creases. Then apply Vaseline to the area. If the rash doesn't clear up, speak to your pharmacist or pediatrician about using an antibacterial or antifungal ointment. Baby powder is useful, too, especially in hot climates. Make sure, however, to tip the powder into your hand, away from your baby, so she does not breathe in any of the dust particles.

GETTING THE RIGHT FIT

Babies come in all shapes and sizes, and sometimes it can be hard to get the right fit. Chafing and rubbing caused by clothes, diapers, and plastic covers can lead to redness and rashes. You'll see noticeable marks along the legs, tummy, and other areas where the elastic or clothes are tightest. You may need to experiment with different brands and sizes to get a better fit.

MEDICATIONS

Sometimes a nursing mom or a baby needs to take medication. Antibiotics have been notorious for causing diaper rash, either through breast milk if the mother has taken them, or directly if the baby has needed them. Antibiotics are a godsend when really needed, but the overprescription of antibiotics can lead to creating more rather than fewer issues, as they kill bacteria both good and bad. Always check with your doctor before taking any medications if you are breast-feeding, and obviously before giving any to your baby. This includes homeopathic medicines and vitamins.

solutions for "heheheh": "i'm hot."

A COOL SOLUTION

My son was born in the middle of winter, so I kept my house toasty warm, with Callum tucked snugly into a bassinet alongside my bed. One night I noticed that Callum had woken saying the word "heheheh." I checked his diaper. It was a little wet, so I changed it and tucked him back in. He said it again a while later.

*I felt his body and found he was hot but not running a fever. I fig-
ured he was just too hot. The room was warm against the cold
night temperatures, plus, he was cocooned in his thick winter
blankets. I removed one of the blankets and turned the heater
down to its lowest setting. He settled back down to sleep.* —SALLY

When you hear "heheheh" in your baby's cry, it means that she is
too hot. If you feel the back of your baby's neck, you will probably
feel whether she is warm. I've noticed something I call "radiating
heat" in hundreds of babies: I'm holding a baby, and she feels as if
she is radiating heat. When you hold your baby regularly, you will be
able to tell when your baby is radiating more heat than usual. You
may think that babies would get hot only in warm climates or during
the summer, but in cold climates and during the winter the risk is
actually higher. Heaters and extra clothing can mean that your baby
can very easily become hot. And new parents often tend to be so concerned that their baby not get cold that they overdress their little one.
Recently, a link has been found between overheating and SIDS (sudden infant death syndrome), so it is very important that you respond
to this sound, "heheheh," appropriately.

In winter, try to dress your baby as you yourself do. If you're
wearing a shirt and a sweater, then your baby will feel fine in those as
well. Add a blanket as an extra layer for newborns, premature, or
young babies. This layer can be easily added or removed without
having to worry about changing your baby's clothes.

When your baby is hot, you obviously want to cool him down.
Start by removing clothing and/or moving him into a cooler place
either within the home, or in the shade if you're outside. In summer or
in hot climates, dress your baby in loose-fitting, lightweight, natural

fabrics, such as cotton. Keep him in the shade or in breezy, cool areas. A baby's skin burns very easily, so it's best to keep him out of the sun. Wet a face cloth and gently wipe your baby's back, body, and limbs. If you have air-conditioning or a fan, be careful not to put your baby directly in front of it; rather, aim to cool the air around him. A tepid bath is always a good way to cool anybody down.

If you are finding that your baby is getting heat rash or redness in the folds of his skin, you may need to review your clothing or heat-prevention methods and take a less-is-more approach. If your baby is showing signs of dehydration such as saying "nuh" (see chapters 13 and 17), requesting lots of feedings, or not producing wet diapers, it's a sign that he has been hot for too long. If you feel the problem isn't improving with the usual methods of cooling down, contact your pediatrician.

solving "horh": "i'm cold."

BABIES ARE VERY SENSITIVE to extremes of temperature. Even on a sweltering day, it does not take much for a baby's core temperature to drop if she is cooled down too much.

WATCH THE VENTS

I was driving one hot summer day, with Emily in her car seat in the back. I had the air-conditioning on, not realizing that it was blowing straight onto Emily. She had started crying and I kept hearing "horh." I pulled over and checked her out. Her little legs were freezing! I felt so guilty. But had I not understood "horh," I might have kept driving, thinking she was just tired. I

wrapped her in a blanket and tucked her back into the car seat.
Once she warmed up, she was fine. –JACKIE

When you hear a long "hhooooorrrrr" in your baby's cry, your baby is becoming cold. You will notice that she will bring her limbs in close, and that the sound is cried relatively calmly. Check her feet and hands first, and warm them up with your own hands before putting on mittens or socks. Only then add clothing, such as a hat or another blanket.

One issue that comes up a lot is cold feet. Parents often forget that feet hang down and need more than socks when the weather gets cold. Often the baby is wrapped everywhere else but is wearing just a thin pair of socks, or in some cases the socks have been kicked off.

If you are in a home that is too cool and you decide to turn on the heater, don't put your baby in front of it, thinking to warm her up. Aim to warm up the air around your baby, rather than focusing on warming her directly. This goes for the heater in the car, too. And remember, the best warming-up system is cuddles from Mom and Dad.

DRESSING YOUR NEWBORN FOR COMFORT

Dressing a newborn can be scary if you haven't done it before or have little experience. They are so small, and it's hard not to think that we will hurt them, or that their heads will not be supported, as we dress them. Babies, however, are tougher then we think, and as long as we are careful, there shouldn't be problems. Your baby will probably protest as you try to dress her, as having things pulled over her head or having her tiny arms pushed through a sleeve can cause even the calmest of babies to become upset. Here are some tricks:

- *Safety first.* Like changing a diaper, it's important to dress your baby in a safe area, where she can't roll off an elevated surface and where there is enough room to spread out a bit.

- *Try to get clothing with snaps, or that opens up.* A cardigan is easier to put on than a pullover, and it is easier to snap a kimono-style onesie around a baby than wrestle with a shirt that has to go over her head.

- *Think in terms of layers.* Her diaper and onesie are one layer, and then a long-sleeved shirt and leggings, or a T-shirt and skirt/shorts, the next layer. In cooler climates, you might add another layer, a cardigan.

- *Pull T-shirts and sweaters over her head first, then put one arm at a time through the sleeves.* Some parents prefer to put on the bottoms along with a diaper change, then place the baby on their lap to change the top half. Others prefer to do it all while the baby's lying down. That's often easier for first-time parents with newborns, especially if they have clothing that opens easily.

- *Hats are good temperature regulators.* Wearing a hat can warm someone up quickly, and taking one off cools a person down just as quickly. It is important that you factor this into your layering, and check your baby to see if she is too hot or cold, saying "heheheh" or "horh."

- *Mittens are often used in summer as much as in winter, although they will be of different materials.* Newborn babies often have remarkably sharp fingernails and love to bring their hands to their face, resulting in scratches and marks. Trimming their nails is difficult and often doesn't stop the sharp scratch. Placing thin cotton mittens over their hands can help prevent scratches to the face. These tend to come off easily, so have a few pairs on hand. In winter or in colder climates, the mittens keep their hands warm. Keep an eye out that they don't lose them.

- *Like hats, socks are good thermal regulators.* They can help to adjust a baby's temperature quickly with a minimum of fuss. In cold weather, make sure you have a heavy pair to keep their feet snugly warm, and in very cold climates, flexible leather shoes work well.

- *Use cheesecloth or a blanket.* Newborn babies spend their first few weeks wrapped in a receiving blanket or being swaddled. A cheesecloth works best in hot climates. Simply place your baby in her diaper and onesie, and wrap her in the cheesecloth. This will keep her contained, so she feels safe but also cool. In winter, have her in a diaper, singlet, fleece pants, or a long-sleeved onesie, and then wrap her in her blanket. Add more layers, depending on the climate and temperature.

PART 3

12-week words

☐

Once you have learned the newborn words and the six-week words, you can move on to the words made by infants who are twelve weeks and older: "gen" for teething, "lowel" for loneliness, "nuh" for thirst, and "augh" for being overwhelmed (although the last can certainly be heard much earlier).

As a baby gets older, gradually creating a working routine will benefit your baby, you, and the whole family. The language can help you do this. Everybody's ability to adapt to change is better when we are well fed, well rested, and feeling safe—and our babies are no different. You've spent the first few months of your baby's life understanding her cries and meeting her needs, so she is likely ready to begin to adapt to small changes in routine, as she has a solid foundation of trust that you can meet her needs.

As a newborn, your baby was at the mercy of her primal reflexes; as she grows, she is beginning to have more control of her body as reflexes subside, change, or integrate into more mature ones. She also has more capacity and reserves—more fat on her body, the ability to take larger feedings, and a more smoothly functioning digestive system. As a result, the intensity of her needs relaxes a bit, and she can go a little longer before urgently needing to have her needs met.

For example, the sucking reflex gradually eases after twelve weeks. Your baby will still say "neh," but the automatic, overwhelming urge to suck will diminish, allowing her to experience a less demanding hunger. The newborn's all-consuming hunger comes from the combination of an immature digestive system with high caloric needs, expressed primally through reflex. These physical responses are slowly diminishing, allowing your baby more, though still limited, control in responding to his hunger. This means that you can slowly extend the time between feedings, or gradually alter the timing if it better suits your family. Always make these changes in increments.

The same goes for sleep. Babies this age are able to stay up a bit longer, without going so quickly from "owh" to the overwhelmed "augh." You can start to slowly shift her bedtime forward or backward, to become more congruent with your family's needs.

The trick is to go slowly, thinking of this process as adapting rather than enforcing. You are trying to adapt your baby's natural pattern into the family's pattern. In my work with families, this gentle adaptation works immensely better than a strictly scheduled, "cry it out" method of enforcing a routine for your baby. You will still put your baby down to sleep when she says "owh" and feed her when she says "neh," but instead of doing it immediately, you might delay just a bit, by offering the pacifier or comforting for an extra five minutes before meeting the need. This does not mean leaving the baby to cry; it does mean that you are encouraging your baby's developing coping mechanisms that naturally grow as she matures. Together, you'll discern her natural rhythms and routines and slowly move toward a more workable and manageable family routine.

By the time your baby reaches this age, you will have already developed your own way of doing things that you know works. You know how to hold her, how to change her, what she likes and dislikes, and so on. Your confidence in meeting these needs is secure. The baby words and solutions in this section are meant to provide you with additional information to add to your existing foundation of words and solutions that you and your baby find effective.

If your baby is twelve weeks old and you're just picking up this book, I encourage you to read about the newborn and six-week words as well. Your baby may still be saying a number of those words—but even if she isn't, you'll find tips and techniques that can help you care for your baby when feeding, burping, changing, and comforting her, and helping her to sleep.

CHAPTER 11

"gen": "i'm teething"

THE TIMING OF THE START of teething can vary, but babies generally start to get their teeth between four and seven months. Some begin as early as three months. No matter when it starts, the effects of growing teeth can be felt (and therefore heard) long before that first tooth appears.

Teething is uneventful for some babies and very difficult and painful for others. This is also true for different teeth: one tooth might come with lots of discomfort, while the next two arrive with none. The pain of teething is often intermittent—it comes and goes for the baby—and parents find this difficult to understand. Since teething usually starts after three months of age, parents hope they've gotten past the worst of the crying and are surprised when their newly smiling angel is screaming again.

When a baby's gums get sore, it natural for her to want to rub or massage the sore area. It is this action that shapes the sound for teething. She will also start to grumble, and in the pre-cry stage you will hear "gen." For babies feeling only mild discomfort, you will hear the word spoken; for a more upset baby, it may be screamed. The baby's discomfort will dictate the velocity and aggression of the cry. Your baby's discomfort will also affect the pitch of this word: more acute pain will result in a higher-pitched, louder sound. So when your baby is crying "gen," you know it's time to help out.

what "gen" sounds like

YOU CAN HEAR SOUNDS similar to "gen" in English words like "hen," "den," and "pen."

To make this sound yourself, pull your cheeks in, between your top and bottom teeth. Then pull your mouth wide into a grimace. Place your tongue behind your bottom teeth and make the motion of chewing, as if you were trying to chew the sides of your mouth. Now vocalize, and you will hear "gen." The sound will vibrate slightly in your nose and palate. It is the chewing motion that produces the "gen" sound—the same motion created by the baby as he adjusts his jaw, trying to relieve the discomfort in his gums.

In addition, you will notice when you reproduce the word "gen" that you half swallow at the end of the vocalization, and then breathe in. This action can produce the "u" sound that follows "gen," which you can sometimes hear the baby make. This "u" sound increases the more upset your baby is—simply because the more upset your baby is, the more he will need to swallow and breathe while repeating "gen" over and over. When "gen" is cried in this fashion, it will sound more like "ugen, ugen," and it is an indicator that the teething pain is more acute.

how "gen" is made

OUR ABILITY TO EAT is supported in part by jaw reflexes that are prompted by the stimulation of our teeth. These reflexes enable us to bite down, keep food in our mouths, and swallow. The reflexes in the jaw also work to stimulate our salivary glands to make and release saliva, which in turn causes us to swallow. These mechanisms operating together are what produce the teething sound "gen."

You probably have noticed an increase in saliva as your baby starts to teethe. This is brought on by your baby's jaw moving in reaction to her sore gums. As she does this, she prompts the jaw reflex that stimulates salivation. (Think of this as the same stimulating motion as teeth grinding, but without the teeth.) The extra saliva will force your baby to swallow. The extra jaw movement also affects your baby's ears, opening up the ear canals, possibly causing her to pull on her ears.

The pressure from the emerging teeth causes her to pull back her lips, flatten her tongue, and pull back the sides of her mouth. She will move her jaw down with her lips over and up, trying to relieve the pressure on her gums. For upper teeth, she will flatten and push her tongue up toward the front of her palate. For bottom teeth, she will flatten her tongue and push the tip toward the bottom front gums. For both upper and lower teeth, the palate is pulled back and open, and the throat is open. Because of the tongue's position, the sound will be pushed more into the nasal cavity, and with the movement of the jaw up and down, the sound "gen" will be produced.

hearing "gen"

WHEN YOU HEAR "GEN" within your baby's cry, you will probably notice other telltale signs that your baby is teething. When you hear this sound, your baby will be chewing—on his finger, on toys, or even you. If you're breast-feeding, you will notice a chewing motion and even a bit of a nip. Your baby is acting upon impulse, not purposely trying to hurt you! When this happens, don't hesitate to replace your nipple with your finger or a chew toy.

There is widespread disagreement among health-care professionals as to whether teething causes diarrhea, a fever, or even real discomfort to the baby. Some doctors will say that teething causes all these things; others will say that it is more likely that your baby caught a cold at the same time, causing these additional symptoms. From my experience, and from what I can hear within a baby's cry, I lean toward the pain of teething being quite individual and very possibly real. Of course, some children are otherwise sick when they teethe, but making general assumptions or speculations about the pain of teething for all infants is not productive. Just as adults have very different experiences when getting their wisdom teeth, so will babies when they teethe. Babies are individuals, and as such, they will have different experiences, all within the spectrum of "teething."

What I do know is that when "gen" is present in your baby's cry, your baby is teething. I also have noted that other physical patterns commonly accompany the sound "gen." As mentioned, these may include drooling, biting, ear pulling, refusal to feed or intermittent feeding, red cheeks, irritability, clinginess, problems with sleeping and wakefulness, diaper rash that may or may not be accompanied by loose stools, and crying.

I have also noticed that on the days when "gen" is cried frequently and in great distress, these associated symptoms appear more readily. Pain in any form is often experienced uniquely by an individual, and it can be accompanied by symptoms such as nausea, diarrhea, headache, anxiety, and other issues. Your baby's pain will be no different: he will have his own unique response to the pain of teething. If your baby is saying "gen," be kind, do what you can to alleviate the discomfort, and remind yourself that it doesn't last forever; it is just part of growing up.

"lowel": "i'm lonely"

Tʜɪs sᴏᴜɴᴅ is almost a universal "lonely" sound for mammals. The meaning is along the lines of "Where's my pack/group/family/Mom or Dad?" You can hear a similar sound in a cat's meow or a dog's whine. You'll hear this sound when your baby needs more hands-on affection.

The reflexes that make the sound "lowel" are particularly interesting, as they blur the line between the emotional and the physical. It may seem that the need for social interaction is an emotional need, but for the infant, it is a physical need as well. For a baby, being part of a caring group of adults is a primal need—a baby left alone faces certain death in the primal world. Babies are innately programmed to want to be close to their caregivers. Studies have shown a measurable hormonal difference between babies who have been held and those who have not—for example, infants in Vietnamese and Romanian orphanages. Of course, in your home, your baby will not be as deprived of contact as these children. However, even your baby will have a primal response when he feels alone, and then the reflex system in his body to prevent his being left alone for too long will be activated.

You may think that "lowel" would be rare in the West, where we lavish attention on our children, but this is actually where I hear it most. We tend to put our babies in separate beds, in different rooms.

We place them in high chairs to feed them, in strollers (often facing away from us) to transport them, and playpens for awake time. We have so much to do in our busy lives that it's hard to find time to just hold our babies. Sometimes our babies just want to look into our eyes, and be held. This interaction is about touching, skin-to-skin contact, and face time rather than toy or color-recognition play. This is simply allowing your baby to get to know you and be comforted by you—by your smell, your touch, your face, and your gaze—and letting yourself do the same with her.

One of the effects of postpartum depression is that the mother may not be able to interact with her baby in this way. Even if she is able to care for her baby physically—changing the baby's diaper or giving a bottle, for example—if there is no eye-to-eye contact or cuddling, the baby will show signs of disattachment.

Children who do not get enough emotional and physical attention are at a higher risk of behavioral, emotional, and social problems. Studies have shown that children who grow up in an environment lacking adequate physical touch and emotional bonding had higher levels of the stress hormone cortisol, as well as different levels of oxytocin and vasopressin (hormones linked to positive emotional and social interactions). Children who were raised in orphanages, even for only eight months, show these differences for years after being adopted into a warm and loving family.

This is why "lowel" is such an important word. It helps us to know when we need to adapt our everyday caring habits to focus a bit more and to be a little more in tune emotionally to our baby's needs. Your baby is saying he needs to be included more in your world. Responding to "lowel" can be as simple as moving him around so he can see what you are doing, talking to him more, or picking him up for a long cuddle.

what "lowel" sounds like

"LOWEL" IS A CRY that is breath-like and sounds similar to a sigh. It sounds like the English words "vowel," "towel," "owl," "howl," and "fowl."

To make the sound yourself, place your tongue behind your top teeth and sigh, adding sound to the sigh. This will produce an "l" sound. Continue vocalizing, relax your tongue, open your mouth almost to a yawn, and then close your mouth. This last part will produce the "owl" sound, which together with "l" makes "lowel."

This word is very rarely heard within a hysterical cry. It's a sadder, more plaintive type of cry. "Lowel" doesn't mean your baby is sad. It just means he's wondering where you are, and expressing that it would be nice to interact with you.

Sometimes you will hear a flutter "lel" before the word "lowel," making it sound like "lelowel." Since your baby doesn't have teeth, her sigh produces a force of air that makes her tongue flutter. When this happens, you'll hear "lel" or "lelel" before "lowel."

how "lowel" is made

THIS PRIMAL CALL FOR ATTENTION is governed by reflexes that affect the baby's endocrine system, glands within the body that govern hormones in our blood. These hormones can be affected by stress, happiness, how well we sleep, aggression, how well we cope with new situations, and how effectively we feel loved, among other factors. Physical touch and emotional interaction have also been demonstrated to affect the endocrine system.

The baby who feels alone will become stressed. Her body's endocrine system reacts in response to the stress, adjusting her levels of hormones, insulin, and adrenaline. This changes the body as an instrument for vocal production, as she slouches and uses only small movements from the diaphragm to produce the air needed for the cry, and makes only small movements with her throat and tongue. You will hear the smallness of these movements in the plaintive sound of "lowel."

We all know what hormones can do to our voices. Certain thyroid gland disorders can cause specific changes to the voice. So it shouldn't be surprising that, driven as it is by the endocrine system, "lowel" sounds different from other cries your baby makes.

hearing "lowel"

GENERALLY, WHEN YOU HEAR "LOWEL," you will have been busy, or you'll realize that the stroller is facing away from you and your baby isn't able to see you, or that you've been a little more physically and emotionally distant than usual from your baby. It is so easy to forget that a baby's world is limited to what is presented *to* him. Even if he is in his crib and you're folding laundry next to the crib, he may be able to see only the mobile hanging above him.

157

"Lowel" will start in the usual pre-cry way, and increase the more distressed the baby becomes. Usually you won't hear a lot of noise before your baby begins to cry "lowel."

Fortunately, this sound is easily solved simply by picking the baby up and giving him some cuddly, quality eye-to-eye contact. If you are hearing "lowel" regularly, you may want to adapt some of your baby's playtime to include more physical interaction with you.

CHAPTER 13

"nuh": "i'm thirsty"

WHEN YOUR BABY IS THIRSTY, you will hear "nuh" within your baby's cry. This typically happens if you live in a hot climate, or even during winter when the heating is on constantly. You also may hear it when your baby is unwell and running a temperature.

Water is one of the most important substances for our health! It helps to transport nutrients around the body, and it removes and dilutes waste for excretion. Water also helps to regulate our body temperature, so a word that lets us know when our baby is running low on H_2O is a very useful thing.

When the human body is low on water, our salivary glands make less saliva, the amount of saliva in our mouth decreases, and our mouth becomes drier. This dryness of the mouth is experienced as thirst. Thirst starts as the salt content of your baby's blood changes and the brain responds by sending messages to his mouth and throat, creating the feeling of thirst. It gives your baby the dry-mouth feeling that lets us adults know we need to drink some water. The baby will use his tongue to spread the saliva around, trying to moisten his dry mouth. That motion helps to produce a "nuh" sound.

Giving water to babies rather than providing hydration only through their milk intake is largely a cultural decision; however, it's usually best not to give water to a baby under four months old. Your pediatrician will have a better idea of what will suit your baby best.

what "nuh" sounds like

YOU WILL HEAR a sound similar to "nuh" in words like "ah," "bah," "rah," and "ha." "Nuh" starts in a very similar way to "neh," which makes sense, as the needs expressed are very closely related. However, because our babies are generally a little older when they begin to say "nuh," and because thirst is a need that develops more gradually than hunger, you will find your baby won't become as upset as quickly when saying "nuh" as when saying "neh."

"Nuh" will start within the pre-cry and will be clear: "nuh, nuh." You will notice that your baby's tongue is sliding back and forth rather than making the clear sucking motion made with "neh."

how "nuh" is made

"NUH" IS CREATED when vocalization is added to the movement of the tongue around the baby's dry mouth. This movement starts similarly to a sucking motion, but the tongue stops halfway behind the top gums and then moves directly down. To make this sound yourself, imagine you are trying to wet your mouth when it's dry. You will notice that your tongue moves back and the tip of your tongue scrapes along your palate behind the back of your teeth. Your tongue forms a kind of scoop shape as it does this. You will feel a natural inclination to swallow, as your saliva glands produce more liquid. As you swallow, your tongue will move along the roof of your mouth until it hits the back of your top teeth, where it next moves down, and then back. Adding a vocalization to this movement will produce the word "nuh."

hearing "nuh"

IF YOU'RE BREAST-FEEDING, addressing "nuh" is simple—let your baby breast-feed. Your breast milk will meet the baby's hydration needs. Breast milk contains enough water, and your body adjusts the consistency of your breast milk based on the needs of the baby. However, if your baby is saying "nuh," you might find she wants only a quick feeding, just enough to satisfy her thirst. Sometimes knowing that in advance can alleviate fears that the baby isn't feeding well.

Bottle-fed babies older than four months or babies who live in hot climates often require water in addition to their formula. Unlike breast milk, baby formula contains extra salts and minerals and is completely consistent in its contents every time (assuming you make it up correctly, according to the manufacturer's instructions). It makes sense that sometimes your baby may need extra water. You will know when to do this by listening to the baby's cries. When your bottle-fed baby is hungry, he will say "neh"; when he is thirsty, he will say "nuh."

This distinction is very important and so helpful for parents who are bottle-feeding their young one, as it takes away the guesswork of knowing whether the baby is hungry or thirsty. Hunger and thirst are two distinct issues, and they are solved in different ways for the bottle-fed baby. Being able to distinguish between the needs and meet them appropriately allows parents to feel more confident in caring for their baby.

CHAPTER 14

"augh": "i'm overwhelmed"

WHEN YOUR BABY IS OVERWHELMED, you will hear "augh" within her cry. When you hear this sound, it means that your baby is overstimulated or at the end of her ability to cope. This sound will mostly be heard within the scream part of the cry, so the pitch will be high and the velocity strong and loud.

"Augh" is based upon the physical reaction caused by stress. It's almost like a precursor to the fight-or-flight reflex we have as adults. It might be part of a protection mechanism designed to scare off predators. The sound is a high-pitched wail—much more sound than you would expect a little animal to make—and it alerts the parents that there is trouble. The sound is usually accompanied by stiffness and jerky movements—perhaps to repel a predator. Although these basic survival mechanisms are no longer needed in our society, they are there, built in for our baby's survival.

Nature is also aware that while these reflexes may help to keep a predator at bay, they could be a problem in everyday life. Nature created an ingenious system to help our newborns not be too stressed. A baby is nearsighted when young, able to focus only on things about eight to twelve inches in front of him. His ability to see color is also limited, and grows only as he gets older and more able to cope with new stimuli. The baby is born with limited movement, again helping to ensure that stimuli are controlled until the baby is older. A baby's need for lots of sleep also helps to protect him from too much stress and stimuli. You will find that poor sleep makes stress and the "augh" word more prominent and regular.

Young babies have a low threshold for overstimulation. They are just getting used to how their body works, to the light and all the sounds in the world, and to the stimulation of physical touch. These stimuli can be overwhelming for even the most robust and placid of babies! When you hear this word, focus on calming the baby down and toning down the stimuli surrounding your baby.

Each baby's threshold for stress is unique and changes based on many variables: how much sleep he's had, how long since his last feeding, whether he's in the middle of a growth spurt, and whether he's feeling unwell, among others. In addition, each baby has his own unique personality and temperament.

We must remember that what we feel comfortable doing in a day may very well be too much for a small baby. It is important to be aware and sympathetic to your baby's stress levels. Even we adults get overstimulated by our world sometimes. Our modern world has far more stimulation than in previous generations: bright lights, blaring TVs, constantly running computers, ringing cell phones, rumbling dishwashers, glaring streetlights, the sounds of cars driving by, flashing sirens, and so much more. If all of this is too much for you at times, just think how easily even a little of it can overwhelm a baby.

Even outings meant to be pleasant diversions for your baby can overstimulate her. In many cultures, babies are kept home for the first month or so, with limited visitors. The focus is solely on parents and baby spending quiet time together, getting to know one another. This gentler approach might suit your baby better.

As soon as your baby starts to say "augh," you know she's reached her limit. This means that you must stop what you are doing and decrease the surrounding stress.

what "augh" sounds like

"AUGH" CAN BE HEARD in words like "lung," "hung," and "young." It is a rhythmical, tonal sound that is repetitive. Unlike the other words, "augh" doesn't have a lot of extraneous sound around the word; rather, the word itself is repeated over and over. One of the key characteristics is the tonal nature of the cry—think of the frustration we express when we say, "Arrrgghhh!"—and the repetitive, almost slow trill produced by the "augh" word.

Trills are sound structures used by many animals to create a sound that can be heard at long range, as opposed to a singular note intended for close-range communication. "Augh" is a slow trill, allowing this sound to be heard throughout the house—or any other place you may be with your baby. It's a sound that gets instant results. Very few people can allow this cry to continue without finding and picking up the baby. When this sound is heard, it elicits an immediate response from other humans.

To make this sound yourself, push your stomach out and hold it there. This will cause you to breathe deeply into the bottom of your lungs. Breathe in and open your mouth, keeping your tongue down and flat. When you vocalize, you will produce an "au" sound. As you close your mouth, you will produce a "gh" sound. When you repeat the motion over and over in succession, you will produce a slow trill, even as you breathe swiftly.

What is interesting about "augh" is how little energy it takes to produce it. There is very little movement in the throat and tongue—perhaps another primal mechanism to conserve energy until the infant is found by the tribe.

how "augh" is made

WHEN YOUR BABY is making this sound, you will see her chin tremble, her body will be stiff, and she will clearly be upset.

The sound is best described as tight and open. The baby's body is usually tight, muscles flexed, but her mouth and esophagus are open. You will find that her arms are held stiffly out in front of her, and it is not uncommon to see her trembling. When you pick her up, her body stays rigid—she doesn't relax and curl her body into you. Usually, you'll hear several "augh" words spoken on each breath.

hearing "augh"

THINK ABOUT A PERSON who is hyperventilating or having an anxiety attack. Something has happened that has alarmed their mind, creating the physical reaction of alertness without focus, rapid breathing, increased heartbeat, elevated temperature, trembling, and often crying. The person is on high alert and may feel nauseous (even actually throwing up).

When we hear "augh" in our baby's cry, we see similar physical reactions, but on a milder scale. A baby's "augh" happens more frequently than high anxiety in adults, and it is triggered by more-ordinary events. You may hear it whenever there's an overstimulus of any kind: the stress of waiting to be fed, being too tired to be able to fall asleep, an overloud or bright environment, the faces of eager relatives wanting to connect with him. It can be a thing or situation that your baby finds overwhelming.

A baby saying "augh" will find it hard to eat, may often spit up, and may wet himself. He may seem hyperalert, which can be mistaken for an interest in playing. Many parents misread this signal, thinking the baby wants to play, and get a huge surprise when their baby suddenly becomes a screaming mess. This is what is meant when a baby is described as "going from zero to sixty in eight seconds."

These overwhelm reflexes seem to dominate other reflexes. During my research, I noticed that when a baby was saying "augh," he did not respond to the palmar grasp or the sucking reflex in the usual way. The bodies of these babies remained rigid, and it wasn't until they were calmed down that those reflexes returned to functioning normally.

Remember this when your baby is crying "augh": you will need to calm her before addressing other needs. As soon she starts to say "augh," know that your baby has reached her limit. This means that you must stop what you are doing and decrease the surrounding stress.

CHAPTER 15

"gen" solutions

WHEN YOU HEAR the word "gen" in your baby's cry, it means that your baby is starting to teethe. This process can be different for each child and for every tooth. You may find that his discomfort comes and goes, especially for the first few teeth. Be kind and gentle—it hurts!—and remember that this is a necessary phase in your baby's growing older, and it will pass.

KNOWING "GEN" HELPS YOU WAIT
OUT THOSE TEETH!

Stacy is my third child, so I was reasonably confident of meeting her needs. She was the usual newborn baby, with a touch of colic around six weeks, but nothing really worrisome. Then at fifteen weeks, she became very unsettled. She no longer slept through the night, and she whined and cried for long periods. I couldn't see any teeth coming through, so I thought she was becoming spoiled, as she was the little sister with two big brothers who were excited about her, and a doting father. I feel bad about this now, but I even left her to cry it out, because it seemed like nothing was solving the problem! Then I learned about the "gen" word. Suddenly everything made sense. I remembered the pain of my wisdom teeth and felt for my poor little one. For some reason, just knowing what the problem was—and that it wouldn't last forever—made dealing with it easier. —TERESE

While she is still in the womb, your baby's teeth start developing as tooth buds within the gums. They tend to break through one at a time, starting with the bottom middle teeth, then the top middle teeth, and then along the sides and back, until by about age three your baby has a beautiful set of twenty baby teeth.

The teething phase is a good time to start your child on the path to good oral hygiene. Your baby will want to bite down on things to ease his discomfort, so make the most of this by introducing items like washcloths and toothbrushes, so he gets used to having something in his mouth. Then, once that first shiny tooth is out, it won't be such a battle to keep it clean by using a washcloth or infant toothbrush.

relief by chewing

GIVING YOUR BABY SOMETHING to chew on will help to relieve the teething discomfort. In Australia, we have hard, fingerlike biscuits called "rusks" that are fabulous for teething. The equivalent in the United States is zwieback, but wherever you live, there will be teething biscuits at your local supermarket.

Other good products are the firm rubber teething rings and teething toys that come in various shapes and sizes. Some are soft and others are hard; some can be frozen and others are ribbed. There are even vibrating shapes that can help to numb the area simply through vibration. Try to purchase a selection of these teething tools ahead of time, ready for when the perils of teething pain hit. You will find that your baby will have a preference, so expect some trial and error as you try out a few different options before your baby finds one that works.

One of my favorite teething toys is simply a toddler toothbrush. The back of the toothbrush is good and chewy, especially the handle, as modern children's brushes tend to have variable grips that are brilliant for biting down upon. The elongated shape is also good for getting into hard-to-reach places, so your baby can push it into the sore part of her gum. They are also inexpensive, so when lost or dropped, you needn't worry. The toothbrush is a good thing to have either at room temperature or frozen. Last but certainly not least, it helps your baby get used to having a toothbrush in his mouth.

Washcloths have more uses than just cleaning dirty faces. Babies often like to chew on the corner during bathtime. Take this further by freezing the cloths and letting your baby have a good chew outside the bath. This can be done with either a dry washcloth or a damp one. Putting some crushed ice inside a dry washcloth and twisting it shut can also be a good teething-pain reliever. The cold helps to numb the gums and the crushed ice to massage them.

You can freeze pacifiers, toothbrushes, and even spoons. If you're freezing a pacifier, use one specially made to do so, or leave a regular one in the freezer for only a short time. If there is any sign of cracking or splitting, throw it away and buy a new one. Toddler spoons are also a good option, as they are thicker and spongier than normal spoons. That said, I have seen many a baby prefer the handle of a cold metal spoon when his gums start to hurt.

When freezing items (even teething rings), aim for a chilled or squishy level of freezing rather than a rock-hard freeze. Baby teething bags can be useful, as they allow you to freeze food items like bananas or other fruits that your baby can chew on, without the worry of your baby swallowing anything too large.

Always make sure there are no holes in or damage to anything you may give to your baby, frozen or otherwise—and beware of anything that could be a choking hazard.

GRIN AND "BEAR" IT

My three-month-old was always "gumming" things, and he was too young for a rusk or toothbrush, so I would freeze his beanbag bear. He loved to chew on his bear! The bean filling massaged his gums, and the cold helped numb them. —TINA

other teething troubles and remedies

TEETHING GEL has been around for years. A gel-type substance that you apply in very small amounts to your baby's gums, it numbs the area of gum where the gel has been placed. It usually tastes terrible, so some babies refuse to allow you to use it. In any case, if you do choose this method, buy a teething gel that does *not* contain benzocaine.

Some doctors suggest children's acetaminophen, ibuprofen, and Tylenol when the pain is bad and certainly if fever is present.

Check with your pediatrician about these options, as he or she will be able to advise on what suits your baby best. If your baby is showing an elevation in temperature or you think that your baby is ill, it's best to seek medical attention, especially with young babies.

GETTING HELP CAN HELP

I was one of those moms who swore to never give her baby medication, but after three long nights of my baby crying, my doctor friend persuaded me to try a bit of commercial pain relief. I wasn't sure Steph needed it, but when I could hear the "gen" word, I knew she was having a more difficult time than most with her new teeth. What a difference! We all got some sleep that night, and she was feeling a bit better the next day. Sometimes a good night's sleep can help everyone.
—GLORIA

Often your baby will show signs of a rash on her face from excess drooling, so be careful to pat her dry, rather than rub, as her skin is very delicate. Use protective creams like lanolin ointment or petroleum jelly to help protect the skin from dampness, if it becomes a problem.

Some babies experience diaper rash when they are teething. Some pediatricians believe the two are linked, and certainly that was true for my son. The minute his bottom got red, I knew the "gen" word would soon follow, along with the inevitable teething discomfort. During these times, it is especially important to make sure you change your baby regularly and use a barrier cream (see chapter 10 for solutions to help with diaper rash).

171

Nighttime waking can be frustrating for parents, especially as it can seem that we have only just gotten our baby into a practical sleep routine when he starts waking from teething pain—but this comes with the teething territory. Even adults have trouble sleeping when they feel unwell. Babies are new to settling themselves into sleep, and sleep cycles are shorter, besides. It doesn't take much to have a baby wake and notice that her gums are uncomfortable. When your baby wakes and you hear the word "gen," you will know that your baby is going to need some extra care and attention. You will also know that this is a temporary situation, which eases the frustration of getting up in the middle of the night. Sometimes all your baby will need is to be helped back to sleep; other times she may need more soothing and relief of her discomfort.

"GEN" HELPS MAKE SENSE OF THE SYMPTOMS

Thank God for the "gen" word. All my children become clingy when they teethe, and I would worry that they were sick or that something was really wrong with them. The "gen" word gives me perspective, and when I can match it up with the other symptoms of teething, such as drooling and the cheek rash, I know what's going on and I worry less. It makes it easier to give them the extra attention and to know how to handle it.
—TABITHA

Most babies become clingy when they are teething, so expect your baby to display an overall unsettledness. It's not uncommon to find your baby wanting to be held all the time, and then fussing while in your arms. It can feel like nothing you do is right, but know that is

172

just your baby feeling unwell. As long as you are there to reassure him, you are doing the right thing. Listen to his cries and vocalizations, and if you hear "gen," you will know he's expressing an overall sense of physical unhappiness, based on teething. Your baby just needs to know you're there.

CHAPTER 16

"lowel" solutions

W HERE'S MY PACK, my clan, my group, my tribe, my posse?"
I struggled with the translation of "lowel" for some time.
We all have a very basic, primitive desire to be part of a group. We
are social animals, and we survive by being part of an organized
social structure. This desire is why we worry that our children may
not be making friends, or feel concern when we meet someone with
few or no friends. We are programmed to find our group, to be part
of a caring society, to look after our families and our extended and
adopted family, and to seek friends within our workplace, neighbor-
hood, and spiritual community.

Our survival depends on us being in a group, and this is even
more important for babies, for without the group's protection, they
will die. With their limited mobility and their dependence on others for food, care, and safety, a baby must always be in the presence
of her clan, and ensure that she bonds to someone who will care for
her, protect her, and help her to grow. That's also why babies are
so cute!

The word "lowel" in your baby's cry means that the baby is not
feeling part of the clan and that he needs more contact with caregivers, with more personal interaction. This can mean more quality
time, not necessarily more quantity. Babies in many cultures are kept
close at hand, strapped to their mothers, or held in close proximity to

caregivers. In our modern society, we tend to focus on putting the baby down on play mats, or in cribs, strollers, and car seats. This can result in a baby who is well cared for but lacking in the primal connection. This lack is what leads to survival upset and "lowel." "Lowel" is not a cry for stimulation through toys, educational play, or distracting objects. This is a cry for interaction with you.

Solving this cry is as simple as picking up your baby and spending more time interacting with her. Babies are generally entertained largely by the world around them. They have their bodies to get used to—not only how they work inside but also how their limbs work—and they use their bodies to take in the world. Babies experience the world through their senses, through taste, touch, smell, hearing, and seeing.

If you find your baby saying "lowel" regularly, and you don't feel connected to your baby, take action. It may be time to see your doctor to talk about how you're feeling. Feeling a little "down" and disconnected is not uncommon for the parent of an infant, but it can sometimes turn into something more serious. Sadness and postpartum depression can be caused by hormonal imbalances, life changes, sleep deprivation, and unfulfilled expectations. Sometimes we all need help.

ways to connect with your baby

ALL BABIES WILL DELIGHT in and need all forms of sensory play and connection. Your baby will love the type of play that covers all the senses: your smell, your touch, your sound as you coo, and your vision as he looks up at your adoring face. But sometimes your baby may have a dominant sense that helps him to feel more connected to you and safe. A dominant sense is a never-fail sense that assures the baby from a primal standpoint that she is not alone. Being aware of your baby's dominant sense and catering to that need is very powerful in addressing "lowel."

In my research for the Dunstan Baby Language, I noticed that the babies who were crying "lowel" were sometimes in the same room with their caregiver, or even in a stroller in a café. Clearly these babies were well looked after, and there wasn't an immediate need such as feeding or changing. So, what was behind this sound? I found in my preliminary studies that a simple change, turning the stroller around so the baby was facing his mom, ended the "lowel" cries. This was what started my investigation into dominant sensory communication, and it does indeed start in the newborn months.

VISUAL WAYS TO CONNECT WITH YOUR BABY

Some babies will need to be able to see you in order to feel connected with you. This means making sure that his stroller, high chair, or bouncy chair is facing you. When other people are holding him, you will need to be standing within sight, or he will start to fuss. If he wakes and the world is dark, a visual child might become scared.

SEEING IS BELIEVING

My baby would be fine—until I was out of his sight. So I used to prop him up in his stroller, and make sure that he could see what I was doing. When he was little, I made sure to stay close, but as he got older I could move farther away. He loved to observe the world, and as long as he had me as an option to observe, he was quite content. —ELISA

Your baby may be able to see only eight to ten inches when first born, but remember, this is nature's divine plan to foster a connection between you and your baby.

Cradling your baby in your arms with his face about eight inches from yours, allow your baby to focus on your features. You will find it hard *not* to engage your baby by smiling and staring back, and this is what you are meant to do. If your baby looks away, don't worry—he is just learning how to connect with you and may be able to do it for only short bursts at a time. This is especially true for premature babies.

Make sure your baby is positioned to be able to look at you as much as possible. The easiest way is to make the most of slings or carriers or strollers that face you, so you can still smile and interact when walking.

As her sight improves, your baby will find things like flowing curtains, ceiling fans, and leaves blowing in the wind fascinating, and will stare for long, contented periods. Move her along with you as you move to different areas of the house. This allows her not only to experience new sights, but it also allows her to see you tackle the day's chores.

When playing with your baby, you will find that high-contrast items and patterns take her fancy. As her vision slowly improves, she will begin to track an item as you move it across her field of vision. Mobiles and small toys with black-and-white patterns are always popular during playtime. Remember, however, nothing is more interesting to a baby than your face and the faces of other friends and family.

AUDITORY WAYS TO PLAY WITH YOUR BABY

Your baby's favorite sound is your own voice, so make sure you talk, sing, and coo to your baby as much as possible. Some babies will be quite contented as long as you are chatting to them. This may sound easy, but it can take some commitment. If you are not a naturally chatty person, or if you're mostly alone with the infant, or if you have a touch of the baby blues, you might find it hard to keep talking aloud. Try narrating what you are doing and why, remembering that your baby understands more than you imagine. It helps to be able to make eye contact with your baby, so it can be easier to have the stroller facing you. Make the best of reading material and singing songs. Sometimes it's easier to read a book aloud than talk to a baby. Simply reading a book out loud to your baby can help your baby feel more connected to you.

GETTING USED TO TALKING ALOUD TO BABY

After I had my daughter, we were alone for most of the day, with my husband working long hours. I realized that I didn't say a word all day, unless I was on the phone. I certainly tended to her, but I felt funny talking to someone who didn't answer. Still, I started to make an effort to explain what I was doing and why, and sure enough, the "lowel" cry diminished. Now when she says it, I know she needs me to talk more. —ABIGAIL

Try to keep the background noise of the radio or TV minimized, so that your baby has a chance to focus on your voice. It's fascinating how we adults innately coo and speak in a higher, more singsong voice when talking to a baby. Our primal knowledge naturally kicks in, as it turns out this is the type of voice babies like to hear most.

If your baby responds best to auditory reassurance, he will need to hear you, even if he can see you. For an auditory baby, you will be able to leave your baby's line of sight for short periods, as long as you keep up the conversation.

Your baby's startle reflex is quite strong, and she will tend to jump and cry at any sudden or loud noise, so it's important to try to be gradual with your sound play. Start talking to her as soon as you enter a room. Bells, bird sounds, and musical tunes will all be interesting for your baby, and if you can add some physical play to it, all the better. For example, you may tickle her back as you both listen to Mozart, or rock her to your favorite Beatles ballad. You may smile within sight of her face as you ring a bell, exaggerating your facial expressions. Always remember: calm environment, calm baby. Listening to angry voices of your favorite TV show or heavy metal rock isn't going to help the baby feel safe.

As your baby starts to grow and make noises, copy the sounds he makes—the cooing, the ahhing. This interaction is important for speech acquisition, not to mention delighting your baby to no end.

tactile ways to play with your baby

SOME BABIES NEED a more tactile approach, feeling most connected when they are being held or touched. It won't be enough to just see you, and your soothing voice will be a poor compensation. What these babies want is to be held constantly. This can be very trying for a tired parent!

FOR SOME, ONLY CUDDLING WILL DO

When I first worked with Priscilla, I was exhausted by my baby's constant crying. But once I found out that he felt safest

being in physical contact with me and I learned the word "lowel,"
I knew that I just needed to hold him for a while to calm and
cheer him. I had been constantly trying to feed him or entertain
him, but I learned from Priscilla that all he really wanted was a
long cuddle. —NADINE

You might be surprised at how little we touch our babies in Western society. We move the baby from crib to playpen to stroller to car seat to bouncy chair, and back to the crib again. Babies are programmed for touch, and many studies show the negative results for your baby when there isn't enough. Invest in a sling or baby carrier that can be strapped to your chest. These not only have the benefit of keeping your baby close to you and near your warmth, your smell, and the sound of your heart and breathing, but they also free your arms to do other things.

Cradle your baby as much as possible, hold him close, and play touching games with him. "This little piggy went to market" is a fun game that, as your baby gets older, will elicit first a smile, then a giggle.

Baby massage has also been shown to improve immunity, so make a ritual during playtime, perhaps after her bath or even before bathtime, if you have a wiggly baby. Lay down a towel and massage your baby's back, legs, arms, and tummy. Don't worry about following any particular massage sequence, or whether you are doing it correctly. This is just about touching your baby. The pressure needed and how much touch will feel good will be different for each baby. Some babies can handle only a minute, while another will lie still for ten minutes (see chapter 9 to learn the basics of massage).

There are babies who never want to be put down, insisting upon being held all the time. My son was one such baby. This can be very draining for the primary caregiver, so do your best to have as much help as possible. Just remember that this need for lots of physical comfort is your baby's personality preference. You might find your-self to be that lucky mother whose teenager is still willing to accept a hug at the school gate.

YOUR SMELL IS IMPORTANT, TOO

Your smell is also a factor in bonding with your baby, so try not to wash with strong-smelling scented soap or wear perfume. Your baby loves and is comforted by his parents' own natural smell. If you're his birth mom, he's grown up inside you and will know your body smell, not a perfume—and for dads and adoptive parents, your newborn will be able to recognize you as his primary caregiver by your natural smell. Skin-on-skin contact with a newborn is especially important—meaning, your baby in his diaper, you without your shirt. Don't limit this type of contact to feeding time; incorporate it into your playtime routine.

CHAPTER 17

"nuh" solutions

N UH" IS THE WORD for thirst, related to but different from "neh," the word for hunger. Initially, the solution for "nuh" is the same as the solution for "neh," especially in a baby who is under four months. However, the word "nuh" has other, very useful applications with both formula-fed and breast-fed babies. Also, recognizing the word can provide reassurance that you aren't blowing your feeding routine just because, on a given hot day, your baby wants to drink a little more milk.

BABY LANGUAGE: A COMMON LANGUAGE
We live in a hot climate and my grandmother, who doesn't speak English, was always concerned about "heat" and the baby. We are originally from Hong Kong, and "heat" in Chinese medicine doesn't mean that the baby has a fever; it refers to heat within the body's energy meridians. My grandmother was always trying to give water to my four-and-a-half-month-old, even after my pediatrician had said to give only limited amounts if she was very thirsty. Once I could explain to my grandmother what cries to listen for, the arguments stopped. If Grandmother heard "neh," she knew the baby was hungry. If it was "nuh," then yes, she would need a sip of water. It made life a lot easier, even in a bilingual home. —MO NE

Just as each baby is different, so each family unit, culture, and environment a baby is born into is different. I have worked with infants around the world, and I tend to rely on the advice of each country's own doctors when it comes to the babies in that country. I feel that their expertise in their own environment is more valuable and appropriate than a dictate from a foreign country.

The word "nuh" is one that elicits very different solutions, depending on the country you come from. In some countries, pediatricians believe that water is fine for a newborn; others will insist on giving no water at all; still others have a middle view of "limited amounts, after four months of age." For the purposes of this book, I will be taking the middle view, which is held generally by American doctors. You may find that your own pediatrician has his or her own views, so check with your pediatrician to see what will suit you and your baby best.

breast-feeding, bottle-feeding, and "nuh"

"NUH" IS A VERY USEFUL word for breast-feeding mothers, as it signals that you need to drink more water. Breast milk can be made using only what you have in your body, and if there isn't enough water, your milk will be rather concentrated. You will notice other physical signs when you might be dehydrated—less letdown during feedings, less breast leakage, or your baby may need to suck a little more to get the milk flowing. If you are expressing your milk, you will notice that there is less volume and that the milk is more creamy than liquid.

Other signs: your baby's urine in her diaper may be a little darker, and you may notice a slight decrease in diaper changes. Your baby's stools may also be less watery and drier, or your baby will need to make more effort to defecate.

If you find that your baby's urine is very dark and/or unusually smelly, or you notice a significant reduction in diaper changes, be sure to speak to your pediatrician.

Make a special effort to drink more fluids, and try to drink during feedings, to replace the amount you are feeding. You will probably need more water than you think. The old saying goes: one glass (of water) for baby, one glass for you, and one glass for your body. Keeping a full water bottle near your breast-feeding chair is usually a good idea.

At the risk of stating the obvious, if your bottle-fed baby is regularly saying "nuh," check the formula instructions. It isn't uncommon for a sleep-deprived parent to read the wrong instructions (perhaps the preparation for an older baby), read the right instructions incorrectly, or change formulas and not read the new instructions. It's worth checking to be on the safe side.

check the environment

"NUH" AND EXCESSIVE BUNDLING
OR HEATED SPACES

I was worried that my baby would get cold, so I bundled him up and kept the heater on. I would often hear the "heheheh" sound signaling that he was hot, but it wasn't until I heard the "nuh" word that I realized why he wanted to nurse so much. He wasn't hungry—he was overheated, just hot and thirsty! —JACQUELYN

If your baby is saying "nuh" frequently, chances are he is in an environment that's too hot, at least for him. This doesn't just mean the tropics. Your home in the middle of winter can be heated to a level to make us all become thirsty. Consider turning down the heat, or take a layer of clothing off your baby and see if that helps.

One place that we often forget can get hot is the car. We may have the car heater on, and the windows let in the sun, further heating the car. The baby is strapped into the cocoon of a good baby seat, which also adds warmth. In my studies on "nuh," the car was one of the most common places where a baby would say "nuh," particularly in colder climates.

If you live in or are visiting a tropical climate, or even a place like New York City in midsummer, the heat can cause thirst not only for you but also for your baby. Do your best to keep the baby cool, and if you take him outdoors, remember you will need to cover him from the sun, as his skin is immature and burns easily.

Formula-fed babies older than four months or who live in hot climates may require water in addition to their milk, for the reasons outlined in chapter 13. When you decide to give your baby water, don't give too much. A few sips when he is saying "nuh" will be enough. This is especially true if your baby is exclusively milk fed—that is, not yet eating solid food. Water is not meant to replace a feeding, just to satisfy his thirst. You will know the difference between hunger and thirst by listening for "neh" and "nuh." You will probably hear "nuh" more often when your baby is in a hot or dry environment, due either to outside temperature or keeping the thermostat set high.

A STORY OF ENVIRONMENT AND ADAPTATION

"Nuh" is a sound that came alive for me when I was studying infant cries in Thailand. While I had heard the sound and knew its meaning, I didn't realize its full impact until it was studied in Southeast Asia. I had arrived in summer, and as the spokesperson for a baby products company, I spent the first week filming with newborns, parents, and pediatricians. It was unbearably hot and humid, especially in costume, wearing makeup, and working under the lights. The babies were similarly uncomfortable, and I noticed that they were saying "nuh" and not "neh," which requires a different tongue action. I know that the reason for this was not a physical difference, as babies the world over have the same reflexes.

I decided this needed further study, and so I conducted several trials during the next eighteen months. I found that while all babies have the same reflexes, and in the same conditions will say the same reflex words, the environment the baby is born into will have an impact on what reflexes are most needed. For babies in Thailand, where it is almost always hot and humid, thirst is their first priority. For breast-fed babies, the solution for thirst and hunger is the same: nursing. As a result, I found that breast-fed babies I studied during the summer in Thailand rarely, if ever, said "neh." The baby would say "nuh"—her priority being thirst—and by default, she would be fed as her thirst was being quenched.

My research showed different instincts with bottle-fed babies in Thailand: for these babies, "nuh" was usually solved with water, and "neh" solved with a bottle. The babies developed a distinct vocalization of the words "nuh" for thirst and "neh" for hunger.

be alert for illness

A BABY SAYING "NUH" is typically just thirsty. However, there are times when thirst is caused by an underlying illness, so it's worth looking a bit more closely if you hear this word from your baby and your intuition tells you something more than thirst might be going on.

Babies who have jaundice (or have a history of jaundice) tend to say "nuh" more frequently. If your baby is running a fever, he's likely to become thirsty and say "nuh." Water in the body helps to regulate temperature, so when our bodies need to cool down, we need more water, particularly when we are perspiring. Elevated temperature and overheating are important issues, so if you feel your baby is sick or has a high temperature, call your pediatrician.

Teething can bring about lots of drooling, causing your baby to lose water that may need to be replaced. If you have administered pain relief, this can also lead to a dryer mouth and produce "nuh." Remember, the sound is created by physical reflex, not conscious thought, so anything that dries out the mouth—meaning that the baby needs more moisture—will create the "nuh" word within your baby's cry.

other physical signs that may indicate the need for fluids

THERE ARE OTHER SIGNS to look for in a thirsty baby. When your baby's fontanel (the depression or soft spot on the top of your baby's head) is depressed, this means that your infant needs more fluid.

Fewer tears are a distinct sign of "nuh" versus "neh." The tear ducts of a newborn are not yet developed, so we don't see tears until your baby is older. By the time your baby is six months old, she will have many tears when crying. When she is saying "nuh," you will notice there will be few, if any, tears. For babies who say "nuh" regularly, you will find their skin is dry.

LISTEN FOR DRY SOUND WITHIN THE CRY

You may notice that your baby's voice is less fluid, and more gravelly when he cries "nuh." This is another outcome of the physical reflex. Even as adults, when our throats get dry, so too do our voices.

CONSTIPATION

It's amazing to me how many people reach for prune juice or over-the-counter infant laxatives to relieve their baby's constipation, before giving the baby plain, simple water. If your baby is constipated, try a little water!

As your baby starts to eat solid foods, you may find that his stools get drier. You may need to add in some water, as by the time he is eating solid food, he will probably be able to start using a sippy cup with a lid. Water can be a big aid in warding off constipation.

water, nighttime sleep, and unavoidable feeding delays

OVER THE YEARS, some mothers have used water to teach a baby to sleep through the night, or to adjust a baby's routine. Giving a small amount of water in a bottle is used in these instances not as a substitute for a feeding but as a tool in order to delay a feeding by ten to fifteen minutes at a time. Babies, like adults, can get into a rhythm that has them hungry at certain times of day. This is fine if it fits with the family routine, but for those times when it needs to be adjusted, especially for babies who like to suck, water in a bottle can relieve their psychological need while allowing their physical need for food to be gradually stretched to a later time. It's similar to adults who have a drink when dinner is delayed; the drink quenches the first pangs of hunger. This practice, of course, should only be done with older babies, with a small amount of water, and only on occasion, so as not to interfere with their nutritional intake.

As with all the words, if your baby wakes saying "nuh," you can be sure that he will simply need a quick sip of water and then will drift back to sleep. "Nuh" is often said by babies sleeping in a hot or dry climate, and this can help them drift back to sleep for an extra hour or two without disturbing their feeding routine.

Offering a little water can also buy you a little time when you're in a pinch and need to delay a feeding a bit—perhaps you need to feed later because you're stuck in traffic and can't get home to breast-feed, or because your breasts need time to replenish, or because you ran out of formula.

what type of water to give?

IT'S BEST not to give a baby water containing fluoride—which means you need to avoid tap water in most Western countries. Filtering tap water or buying bottled water will solve this problem. If you buy water, make sure to buy a nonmineral type, with a low salt content.

Check the sodium level on the label. Many mothers prefer to boil the water first to sterilize it, which is a helpful safeguard for young babies. However, after your baby is about six months old, filtered and bottled water will be fine.

Give your baby room-temperature water. Water that's too hot or too cold might be rejected, and too-hot water can scald your baby's mouth and throat. Even water that may be okay for you in temperature can be too hot for a baby, so if in doubt, cooler is better than warmer, as babies are easily burned.

Use a bottle—or I've seen some nurses use a spoon, particularly for breast-feeding babies. You will not be giving a lot of water, just a few sips to start. This is not a replacement for a feeding. When your baby gets older and is eating solid foods, water becomes a beverage, given in a sippy cup. For an older baby, limiting the amount become less important.

"Nuh" is an interesting word in that, until the baby is four months old, the solution is simply awareness. It may give you the knowledge that you need to increase your own water intake if breast-feeding, or that your baby may want to have a few short feedings during a hot spell of weather, or that the heat is set too high in your apartment. Primarily, though, when the baby is less than four months old, the solution is simply to feed her. As she gets older, you may start to offer water, but even then, the intake is rather small. If you do find that your baby is excessively thirsty, and you have made all the usual adjustments, visit your doctor to rule out any other concerns.

CHAPTER 18
"augh" solutions

A UGH" IS THE WORD for "overwhelmed," and you will hear this word in your baby's cry when he is overstimulated, overtired, or just at the end of his tether. When you hear "augh," act quickly, as this sound can tend to feed on itself, creating a spiraling effect that is hard for your baby to stop.

The first thing to do is to remove him from the stimulation to help him calm down. Once he's less frantic and starting to wind down, you can begin to address the reason for his feeling of being overwhelmed.

TOO MUCH, TOO SOON = OVERWHELMED BABY

I played classical music to my baby in the womb, and when my son was born, I had a whole program organized of things I thought we could do together—listening to classical music, reading stories, playing outside, doing arts-and-crafts projects, et cetera. I didn't realize you don't start doing those things when they are newborn! When my son cried, I thought he was bored, so I increased the outings, the stories, and so forth. Things got so bad that he found it hard to go to sleep, hard to eat, and he just seemed to cry all the time. After learning about "augh," I realized he was overstimulated. I started doing calming holds and activities—things like just letting him lie in my arms and explore his fingers. The difference was dramatic: after only three days,

he was a different baby. He cried so much less, fed better, and
slept a full six hours each night! —GENEVIEVE

One of our most basic, primal reactions is the fight-or-flight
response. This reaction is an important safety reflex, built in for our
survival. Even though nature has provided our infant with mechanisms to protect him from overstimulation, a baby can't move and
therefore can't escape (flight) from overstimulation. It's up to us to
create an environment that has the right balance of calm and excite-
ment for our baby—and we tend to forget just how stimulating and
overwhelming the world is for a little one.

It could be that you are in a room full of people, that the TV is too
loud, or that it's simply the end of a long day and a bath is just one
more change that's too much for your baby to cope with. Or it could
be that he is being passed around and held by too many hands. Or
maybe other children keep trying to hold the baby's hand, or he's been
in the same position for too long. Lights can be distracting but they
can also be overwhelming—babies spend a lot of time on their backs,
looking directly into overhead lights. Low light can be comforting.

Responding to "augh" helps you and your baby establish a good
practice of paying attention to needs. In time, your baby will be able
to internalize that and learn to regulate himself: when things are "too
much," we can take a time-out to gather ourselves. You are not spoil-
ing your baby by responding to his needs; you are setting an example.

When your baby says "augh," it doesn't mean that he'll always
need to have quiet, or that he'll never like being in a room full of relatives. It means that at this time, at this stage of development for his
age, with this set of circumstances, he's had enough.

When your baby is saying "augh," you need to move him away

from anything that may be overstimulating him, either by removing the stimulus or by moving the baby to a quieter area.

grandma knows best: primal calming

WE ALL KNOW of grandmothers and nurses who can pick up any baby and instantly stop the crying. I myself am able to do this; it isn't a hard thing to learn. Babies pick up on the confidence level of those in contact with them. They're also looking for reassurance. You can think of this as a variation on the primal dominance idea. The defenseless baby wants to know that he is safe, and the strongest, most confident person—the dominant adult—is most likely to be able to keep him safe. A baby will know whether the person holding him is unsure or scared; he will feel tentative hands and a rapid heartbeat.

Once held, a baby won't differentiate between his own rapid heartbeat and that of the person holding him. This is why the calming methods below start with a fast, matching heartbeat or rhythm. The thinking here is that the perceived threat to the baby's wellbeing will diminish as he feels the adult's decreasing heart rate and slowing motions.

Nurses and grandmothers who have this gift tend to be firm and calm when they pick up a baby. The baby instantly responds to this confidence, feeling he is being held by someone who knows what to do and has things under control. Even if the baby keeps crying, you will notice that the nurse will not hesitate, intuitively standing up, patting the baby's back, and rocking back and forth. She will start the rocking rhythm faster, slowing as the baby calms. This method of primal calming is repeated worldwide, in many different cultures.

THE AGE-OLD METHOD: THE HEART HOLD

- Hold your baby up against your chest, over your heart, with your left hand supporting your baby's body and the other holding her against your body. If she is stiff, you will need to hold her firmly, using your fingers to support her neck and stop her head from dropping backward.
- Breathe deeply in and out, pushing against your baby. Make it deliberate, and start by matching your breathing rhythm to your baby's rapid breathing.
- Once matched, bring your breathing down to a slower rate, and your baby will follow.

USING RHYTHM

- Holding your baby snugly to your chest, position your feet with one foot in front of the other.
- Rock back and forth, starting with a fast movement; then slowly reduce the speed of the movement. Be conscious of the rhythm, going from fast to slow, matching the baby's movements, and slowing them down.
- Follow the same principle when gently patting your baby's back or bottom, again starting at the speed of your baby's movements and slowing the speed to a calm pace as your baby slows down.

Rhythmically, pass your hand slowly down over his forehead and over his nose, gently closing his eyes. Repeat in a very slow, gentle way, until his eyes close and he calms down. This motion can also be replicated from the forehead over the back of the baby's head. For babies who respond to this motion, try the same movement down his back along his spine, as well as on the soles of his feet and on his hands.

SOLVING "AUGH" BUILDS YOUR CONFIDENCE AS A PARENT

I used to feel uncomfortable holding my baby and would hand her off to the nanny whenever she cried. It was really embarrassing that my baby seemed to prefer a stranger to me! Once I learned to breathe and rock to the rhythm of my baby, and then slow down my breath and rocking as she slowed her breathing, I was able to calm her crying! I called it my "augh" dance. Now when I hear "augh," I pick her up and stand with her, rocking and breathing in rhythm. It works like a charm—and I'm not feeling so inadequate. —STACY

reduce the stress, not the connection

BABIES HAVE DIFFERENT STRESSORS, and different stress thresholds, from adults. In my work with families, I often see otherwise attentive, sensitive parents who have trouble recognizing stress in their baby, and even more difficulty identifying the source of their baby's stress. Below are what I've found to be the most common— and most "missed"—stressors for babies, with tips for addressing them using your comforting connection with your baby. Attending to these might help you when your baby says "augh."

TOO MUCH INTERACTION

While babies are innately programmed to bond with their caregivers, there can be too much of a good thing. Too many people holding, looking at, and wanting contact with baby can be overwhelming. The younger the baby, the more you will see her react strongly to this stressor. This doesn't mean you can tell your mother-in-law not to visit (nice try!), but it does mean that you should schedule her visit after your baby is rested and fed. It also means that you can (gently) insist that the visit take place in your home, so when you see that your baby's had enough, you can move her into a calm space—ideally, before she winds up into "augh." By controlling both the environment and number of people involved, you have set up the visit for success for both Grandma and baby.

SENSORY OVERSTIMULATION

Sensory overload is particularly common in infants. Often, what we adults would consider normal is too much for a baby. Here are some examples:

- *Auditory stress.* Too much noise may include high-energy music, TV, the sound of many voices, air-conditioning units, sirens, and so on.
- *Visual stress.* Visual stressors may include overhead lights, lamps, mobiles, the TV, sunlight, bright colors, moving items, activity of siblings, friends and relatives, too many faces smiling and engaging the baby (especially if they're visitors), a period of eye contact that's too long, and more.

- *Tactile stress.* This can come from being passed around to too many people, wearing uncomfortable clothing, being too long in the car or in the vibrating baby swing, children touching the baby, to name some.
- *Body or internal stress.* Your baby may become stressed from waiting too long between feedings, not sleeping long enough or having missed his sleep time, the temperature or the weather, where or how he's sitting or lying, or sometimes even being out of his home environment for too long.

HEADING OFF "AUGH" BEFORE IT HAPPENS

My baby was very affected by her own body's needs—internal stress. I learned that if I needed to go out to run errands, I had to do it after her nap, diaper change, and feeding. If I tried to stretch the time out until her next feeding, she would become so upset that it was impossible to do anything! As I became conscious of timing and made sure she had what she needed so she didn't get overwhelmed, the hysterical outbursts of "augh" didn't happen. —TONYA

more strategies for solving "augh"

CALM ENVIRONMENT, CALM BABY

We modern mothers are programmed to believe that we should be up and about quickly, even if we just gave birth. We tend to believe that we should be as active with the outside world as we were before the birth of our child, almost right away. While you may be ready to get back to the world, it's important to be sure your baby is ready, too. It is not unusual for a newborn to become overwhelmed just by leaving his home! The new sounds and lights will be exciting at first, but very quickly can become too much. My own son could handle only short outings, and even then, only one per nap cycle.

While it may seem as though your baby's life is boring, she is very busy learning how to be in her body and how to make that body work. She also needs to learn the new skills of eating, sleeping, and bonding with her mom and dad. All this, plus getting used to being in the big world outside the womb, is your baby's full-time job.

BREAK THE CYCLE

Often the baby winds himself up into a frenzy of crying and is unable to calm down. When this happens, a change of scenery or environment can help to break the cycle of crying, allowing you to fix the problem and help your baby to move on.

CHANGE THE ATMOSPHERE

A change of temperature and airflow on his face can help break a baby out of his "augh" pattern. You can try walking outside, which alone can be enough to help your baby refocus. You can replicate this inside by walking in front of the fan, or even opening the freezer door. Try blowing in his face, or even covering his eyes gently with your hand. The aim is to break the cycle of the upset, and once it's interrupted, to step in quickly with the settling techniques we've discussed. There won't be a long pause, so make the most of it when it comes.

USE SOUND

Some types of noise can be very useful in breaking the cycle of "augh," as well as soothing the baby afterward. Simply saying "shush, shush" can be enough, but I have heard many stories of the sound of vacuum cleaners, dishwashers, or air conditioners lulling a baby to sleep. Noise machines are popular, as they have a number of different settings, as well as atmospheric sound tracks. You may find your baby loves to fall asleep listening to ocean waves, rain falling in a forest, or simple "white noise." Some babies like to hear Mom's and Dad's voices: sing a few lullabies.

THE BELLS DID IT

The problem for us was breaking the cycle of "augh." The breakthrough came one day when my three-year-old started shaking her set of percussion bells. It was enough of an interruption for her screaming baby brother to catch his breath—and then the rocking and patting actually worked! Without the bells, it would take ages for him to have a break in crying. –DAVID

WATER

Running the shower is a good cry breaker, as the sound is soothing and the steam provides a great change in atmosphere. Also, bathrooms tend to be small, with limited additional stimulation—no TVs, toys, crowds of people. You don't have to bring the baby into the shower; usually just being in the bathroom with the shower running is enough. And if you feel a lullaby is called for, everyone's voice sounds better in the shower!

SHOWERED WITH LOVE

Terry would say the "augh" word in the afternoon, especially when he had been at day care. I would bring him home and he would cry and cry. The shower was the best way to settle Terry. I'm not sure if it was the sound, the steam, or maybe the positive ions in the air from the running water, but it always worked.
—ALISON

settling "augh" with motion

STROLLERS

Strollers can be a godsend for the parents of an upset baby. The stroller allows you to quickly transport your crying baby into another environment, creating a change of atmosphere to help break the cycle. It also enables you to use the power of motion to settle the baby. Moving the stroller back and forth can create a great rhythm for comforting an upset baby. As with the settling holds described above, start with a fast motion that mirrors your baby's heartrate, breathing, and crying; then slowly bring the motion down to a slow back-and-forth.

Consider facing the "augh" baby toward a dark area (if at night) or placing a receiving blanket over the front of the stroller. This will help minimize distractions and decrease excess visual stimulation—both will help with the calming.

BOUNCY CHAIRS OR BOUNCINETTES

Bouncy chairs come in a variety of styles and shapes. There are simple ones that you can bounce with your foot, or that your baby can bounce herself when she gets older and can kick her legs. There are seats that rock front to back or side to side. For those who have other children (and other responsibilities), consider deputizing an older child to help with the bouncing—just make sure that child is mature enough to handle the job safely. Or consider an electric swing or seat. The cost of the batteries is well worth the calm, particularly if you've been dealing with a crying baby for some time and are feeling overwhelmed or "augh" yourself!

THE CAR

I know many families who drive their way to a calm baby. This method is easier in the United States, where infant car seats can be removed from the car; in many countries, parents need to remove the baby, not the car seat, from the car, which can restart the crying after a soothing drive. Using the car whenever your baby is upset probably isn't practical, but it's a good strategy to keep in mind when other options don't work.

WEARING YOUR BABY

I had a very ingenious mother tell me that yoga poses worked on her baby—not yoga for the baby, but yoga for Mom while wearing the baby! Apparently the extreme movements helped to break the cycle of crying, and the motion and closeness to Mom helped to keep this baby calm. This same model can be replicated while on a treadmill, exercise bike, or simply walking with your baby strapped to your chest. Of course, you want to be careful to make sure her neck and head are protected and stabilized, and not to do anything that would create a shaking motion.

SUCKING

The motion of sucking can help calm your baby, but offering a pacifier works best after you have broken the crying cycle. Try a few different methods until a break happens. Once it has, pop in the pacifier or breast (if you are trying to increase milk production) quickly, before he becomes upset again.

SWADDLING

Sometimes reducing your wailing baby's motions can help comfort him when his body movements have become jerky. Either hold the baby snugly, or wrap or swaddle him (see chapter 5). This will help to calm the startle reflex, should it happen as he calms down. Infants are familiar with the cramped quarters of their mother's womb, so the sense of feeling contained, in this case by a blanket or your arms, helps them to feel more secure.

CONCLUSION

M Y SON is the most wonderful of children, but there was an occasion a while ago when, as happens to most of us at one time or another while growing up, he ended up in the principal's office. When he was told that they planned to call his mother, he said, "Good. I think she should be here." When the principal relayed this story to me, I couldn't help smiling. It showed me that when Tom was in trouble, he knew I would be there to support and help, and he felt safe no matter what the circumstances.

I like to think that understanding your baby's language from the day she enters the world is the beginning of the trust we all long to have with our children. I have seen this longing firsthand when working with parents. From suburban couples to members of a bike gang, from Turkish tobacco growers to Hollywood starlets, refugee women to UN diplomats, teen gang members to everyday housewives—we all have something in common. We all want our children to grow up to be happy, healthy, productive members of society. We all hope to have a close relationship with them long after they have had their own children. We are all parents, and regardless of our circumstances, we can all be great parents and raise happy, well-adjusted children. It can start on day one, with feeling that we know how to address our baby's needs. It is my dearest hope that understanding your baby's cries will be the first step to a lifetime of positive communication and bonding between you and your child.

THE WORDS CHART

WORD	TRANSLATION	SOLUTION
"neh"	"I'm hungry."	feeding
"eh"	"I have wind."	burping methods
"owh"	"I'm sleepy."	help go to sleep
"eairh"	"I have gas."	gas relief methods
"heh"	"I'm uncomfortable."	change position
"heir"	"My skin is irritated."	relieve rash or other irritation
"heheheh"	"I'm hot."	cool down
"horh"	"I'm cold."	warm up
"nuh"	"I'm thirsty."	water
"gen"	"I'm teething."	chewing
"lowel"	"I'm lonely."	more interaction
"augh"	"I'm overwhelmed."	calm down

about the research

DISCOVERING REFLEXES

It took more than three years after I had classified the sounds for me to work out that they were associated with infant reflexes. I had been trying for years to find the physical reason for why the sounds were made. I had been asked to release the classification to the public but had not felt comfortable doing so until I had found out how the sounds worked. How could all babies, regardless of race, culture, or circumstance, be making the same sounds, having the same meanings? The enthusiastic nurses, parents, and practitioners using the system believed it was a "spiritual" language, but I knew there had to be a reason that was clear and understandable, and I was looking everywhere to find it.

Coincidentally, I had been studying retained primitive reflexes, just out of my own interest, and taking an anatomy course, also for fun. I'm severely dyslexic, so I have trouble remembering letters, numbers, or anything in order, and I have to use as many different modalities as possible to learn. Since I was studying anatomy, I decided to get a massage, and was using the time for tactile learning, repeating the names of the muscles and bones in my head as the masseuse worked. The woman giving me my massage was very vocally expressive—she laughed loudly, sneezed when the heat-treatment machine started making steam, and yelped when she stubbed her toe. These adult displays of sound and reflexes gave me an idea: perhaps the sounds I was hearing in babies' cries were actually linked to reflexes. I raced off to see if I could find a link.

The first word I looked at was "neh," the word for hunger. I knew babies certainly had a sucking reflex. I looked closely at the babies I had filmed for the word "neh," especially at their mouth movements before the pre-cry phase, and I compared what I saw with the babies saying other words. I had noticed that babies after the age of four months continued to say "neh" in their cries only if a caregiver had responded to "neh" when they were newborn. Why would a sound be present in every baby's cry during a short period, then disappear if not addressed? The change in a newborn's sucking reflex corresponded with this age and change.

As I started to look at other primitive reflexes and words within cries, I found that they, too, matched up. I conducted further study, making sure the infants in the study had passed all the basic health reflex tests. Once the sucking reflex was elicited either by a finger or pacifier, we would record the cry and see how many babies produced a "neh."

Knowing the physiological reason why the baby was making the sound not only validated the words but also helped explain why the sound is made, and directed us toward solutions. Some words were easier to link to reflex than others. "Heh," the word for "uncomfortable," was tricky. How could one sound mean such different things? Being hot is the opposite of being cold, and what does diaper rash have to do with it? It wasn't until I researched the skin, the stimulus felt by the skin, and the consequence to muscles and movement, that

I started to see how that worked. The skin was the receptor, the informer, and the catalyst to other reflexes.

"Owh," the word for "tired," was easier, simply because one of the methods we use in singing opera is to yawn. The sound produced when singing with one's mouth in the position of a yawn enables the singer to produce a perfect note. It is also very easy to replicate, and babies display the reflex easily.

My basic process in seeking these connections was to listen to raw footage of infants crying and allow my mind to pick up a pattern. I would hear a "sound signature" repeated within a number of cries. I would isolate the sound and then see if I could replicate the conditions to have the infant re-create it. From there, we moved to intervention trials (see "Researching the Discovery," below).

Of course, there were always doubts and variables, and in these cases I went straight to the source and back to my skill of hearing. I sat with crying infants, and I listened. Often when I did this, I was able to hear nuances of sound information that didn't come through in re-cording and playback.

DISCOVERING THE DIFFERENCES

When I went to the Cry, Colic, and Sleep Clinic at the Brown Center for the Study of Children at Risk at Brown University to work on writing the protocol for formally testing the infant classification, I was surprised at how differently I had approached the subject of infant cries, compared to traditional academia. I realized I had taken a nonstandard approach quite different from that of current cry researchers.

First, I was looking at the entire vocalization, starting with the baby's pre-cry vocalizations through the baby's full screams. Other researchers were ignoring the pre-cry and focusing on the screaming part only. In addition, these researchers focused on the cry as a whole, whereas I focused on sounds heard within the cry.

I believed that a baby's cry had meaning—I guess because I was a mother. If a cry had meaning, then I believed there had to be an indicator within the cry that would tell me what it meant. In prehistoric times, an infant's cry would have alerted a predator to a weak and helpless animal, so I theorized that nature would have balanced that risk with a function that was useful to the species. To me, that meant information about the baby's needs. Evolution would not make such a fundamental mistake—a species whose vulnerable offspring alerted predators to their location—without an associated benefit. For an infant's crying to be positive for humankind, it would make sense that the cries had meaning and enabled the parents to care for their offspring.

This line of thinking is what led me to analyze the pre-cry sounds. It would be critical to care for a baby's needs before he began to cry in earnest and alert any predators. The pre-cry's quiet vocalizations could accomplish that.

When I traveled the world to analyze baby cries and parenting practices in comunities with tribal attributes, I noticed that babies didn't scream as much as they did in Western societies. This finding further fueled my belief that pre-cry vocalizations are informative and intended to be preventative communications.

I had grown up with many animals, and I had observed that within animals' sounds, there were understandable meanings. Cats had certain meows that had different meanings; dogs had different barks and whimpers for different issues, as did horses and cows.

These sounds were neither from language nor from huge intellect, yet they were understandable as communication. I believed that there might be a human equivalent to a dog's bark or a cat's meow, voiced before we acquire knowledge or control over our bodies, yet having meaning—an innate way of communicating built into us as a legacy of more primal times.

As my research continued and I was able to isolate sounds within an infant's cry that corresponded with specific needs, it became evident that babies' cries were physically based, not emotionally based, as was traditionally believed. This meant that rather than a baby crying because she wanted something (emotionally based), there were clear physical associations between the babies' needs and their cries.

This finding also conflicted with the traditional view that infant crying is nonspecific; that is, that there's no differentiation in babies' cries based on their various needs. My findings show that babies do have specific reasons for crying, that the cries are specific to certain needs, and that parents can quickly learn to differentiate between the cries and therefore better answer those needs.

RESEARCHING THE DISCOVERY

When I began my intensive research, I spent hundreds of hours with parents and their babies, listening to the baby, watching how the parents responded, suggesting responses that I felt were appropriate to the baby's need, and getting feedback from the parents as to whether my suggestions helped. I would then leave the parents for a period of time with the tape of the words and my suggested solutions.

The next step was to start taking myself out of the equation. The language needed to be understandable on its own without personal explanations or input from me.

We began intervention studies, which involved three groups. Group one was given the correct translation of a given baby cry; group two, the incorrect translation; and group three, no translation. Groups were selected using random-sampling methodology. Within the groups, the mothers and babies were tested randomly for different words, different solutions, and at different times of day. The process involved around sixty babies over the course of a weekend, and was repeated with different samples and at separate geographical locations over the course of a few months. Every intervention was videotaped, classified, and added to the already very large body of evidence that was growing to support the idea of words within infants' cries.

I also wanted to find out if this classification was universal to all infants. I bought many, many secondhand video cameras and tapes, and sent one to everyone I knew who was going overseas. I asked them to go to the countries' local midwives to record infants crying! I also asked hospitals around the world to send me recordings. I was able in this way to hear the sounds of babies from many other parts of the world and establish the basis for consistent universal patterns in babies' cries. I then conducted observational research in a number of countries, including the United States, Sweden, Turkey, New Zealand, Tahiti, and Australia.

The study continued to grow, with input from researchers, professors, and universities around the globe. The most personally meaningful input was contributed by the professors working at Brown University's world-renowned Cry, Colic, and Sleep Clinic, also called the Colic Clinic. Professors Linda Legassi and Barry Lester were amazingly generous with their time and advice. They came to Australia to see how my research was being conducted, spent hours reviewing the results, and then invited me to visit them in Rhode Island. There, they taught me how to conduct tests and research measures, and we spent many months writing the protocols for the infant language and working with researchers from many universities on ethics and research implementation.

This effort resulted in an independent study that was conducted in Australia, the United States, and the United Kingdom. This study was not the full protocol originally written but a simplified version, constrained by the parameters of international logistics and funding.

Independent studies conducted in the United States and Australia by Leading Edge focused on two objectives. The first was to validate that parents could learn to precisely identify sounds within their infants' vocalizations. The second was to establish the effectiveness and immediate parental outcomes of using this language system. Studies were conducted in the United Kingdom by 2CV England using the same parameters and producing similar results.

The control and test group samples were matched, and composed of two cohorts. Each group was ethnically diverse and contained a mix of first-time and experienced mothers with healthy, full-term infants. Standardized self-report measures were used to collect data and consisted of the Maternal Self-Esteem Inventory and the Parental Stress Index, both easily understood by a mix of language and educational levels.

Group one was given a DVD containing only solutions—as in how to burp your baby, feeding holds, and the like. The other group was given a DVD with the same information, along with the addition of the language. The solutions in the solution-only DVD were modified to make the DVDs in each group the same length, and thus the same amount of time in "helpful" exposure.

The results spoke for themselves:

- 90 percent of all mothers thought that the ability to understand and recognize the five distinct sounds babies made when crying was very beneficial.
- 100 percent of first-time mothers reported it highly valuable.
- 70 percent reported their babies settled faster.
- 50 percent of mothers experienced more unbroken sleep.
- 70 percent reported feeling more confident as a mother and experienced greater self-esteem, a reduction in stress, and a feeling of being more relaxed and in control.
- 50 percent of mothers felt a deeper bond with their babies.
- 50 percent experienced better feeding.
- 67 percent of fathers reported reduced levels of stress and a more positive marital relationship as an immediate result of greater paternal involvement.

And this research was conducted with just the bare minimum of five sounds and minimal solutions and explanatory information.

The results were so amazing that it caught the attention of the media, and I appeared on numerous national TV shows. Baby magazines, papers, and journals did features, and radio was abuzz with activity.

DISCOVERING INTERNATIONAL DIFFERENCES

As the language became more popular, I was afforded the opportunity to travel for research, consulting, and philanthropy. I was able to conduct baby language research in places I had only dreamed of visiting. The biggest finding from Thailand was the word for thirst, "nuh." During my time there, I found that I wasn't hearing "neh" as

much as usual, but another sound: "nuh." The babies who were saying "nuh" responded happily to being fed. They didn't say "neh" in
their home settings, but were saying "nuh" regularly. It was unbe-
lievably hot during my first trip to Thailand. I noticed that the babies
who came to the air-conditioned studio were saying "neh" in the air-
conditioned room. This led me to consider circumstance and sound.
Babies can all say the same sounds, but these sounds are dictated
by need.

When I spoke with Thai midwives and pediatricians about this, I
found they were well aware that babies had separate needs of thirst
and hunger. My further research into infant cries and international
parenting techniques led to additional sounds being added to the
language.

Each country that I go to requires study. I may be translating the
same sounds, but they need to be translated into another language,
another environment, and a different set of parenting beliefs and
family dynamics. In some cultures, the children are left with the
grandparents while the parents work, returning on the weekends. In
other cultures, the mother raises children, with the father going to
work. In still other cultures, parents bring baby to work with them.
These customs profoundly affect how I teach the language. How I
explain something to a seventy-year-old Korean grandmother will be
different from how I work with a young working mother in the
United Kingdom or the United States, or a father in Indonesia.

There are also differences in how children are viewed in the social
hierarchy of a community. The birth of a boy could cement the position of the mother in a family household, giving her standing and
respect. In some cultures, I found myself teaching the words to the
mothers of boys, as the birth of her son gave her the status to decide

how to raise the children. In a family with only girls, the mother-in-law made many of the parenting decisions, and she was the one to learn and use the baby language.

Language also plays a role. In Thailand, there is no word for burping, so the translation for "eh" became "to chase away the wind." This translation developed from the Buddhist philosophy of good air and bad air. A Thai mother understands the need to chase away the bad wind, which dovetails nicely with the idea of getting rid of an air bubble that causes the baby discomfort.

Religion needs to be considered as well. Balinese Hindu parents believe their baby's feet shouldn't touch the ground for the first one hundred days; therefore, babies must be held constantly by family. Babies that are held all the time generally have less gas, so I didn't need to spend much time on "eh" or "eairh" with Balinese families.

The environment the baby is born into can have a huge impact on what words are heard in the baby's cry. New Yorkers are amazing in how they take their newborns everywhere, even on the subway! I make sure to teach New York parents "augh," the word for "overwhelmed," as I know they will need it. In Norway, a place with a more laid-back pace, I tended to hear "augh" less frequently, though I did hear a lot of "owh" ("I'm tired"). Where I was staying, it didn't fully get dark even in the middle of the night, which affected sleep routines and rituals. In countries like Japan, space is limited, with often only one room for all aspects of family life. Beds are rolled out at night and rolled away during the day, and infants are surrounded by family nearly all the time, even at night. They don't need to cry very much or very loudly to have their needs met. I found these families quickly tuned in to the baby's pre-cry vocalizations, hearing the words easily. All of these differences contribute to the type of parenting care the baby will receive, and influence the words most commonly said and addressed.

Customs about childbirth and parenting have a physical effect on the infant, affecting the words commonly heard within a baby's cry. As mentioned, in cultures in which babies are constantly held in upright positions, the babies experience a lower instance of colic and reflux. In cultures in which the mother and baby are sanctioned to spend quality time together without interference from work or a constant stream of visitors, breast-feeding comes easier. Co-sleeping cultures report fewer sleep problems and less sleep deprivation compared to those that follow a sleep standard of separate rooms. And those cultures in which extended family plays a parenting role tend to show less postpartum depression—a dangerous problem for mothers that can impede their ability to respond to their babies' cries.

Through my travels and research, I discovered that understanding baby cries is as much about understanding the ecosystem of the family and listening to parents as it is about understanding the baby's ecosytem and listening to the baby.

In the end, I found that, as much as I was able to help families around the world by teaching the language, they were able to help me equally or more in coming to a better understanding of how babies, parents, families, and communities all combine to create a caring web where our youngest can grow and thrive.

INDEX

allergies
  to disposable diapers, 130
  formula and, 63, 125
  intestinal gas from, 112
  mother's diet and, 122, 136
  new foods and, 137
  to toiletries and laundry products,
    136, 137–38
"augh": "I'm overwhelmed"
  breaking cycle
    of upset, 198
  calm environment, 191–93, 197–98
  calming methods, 194–95, 198–202
  primal calming, 193
  sound signature and visual cues,
    162–66
  stressors, 195–97

Babinski reflex, 17
baby carriers. *See* slings or carriers
baby language. *See* Dunstan Baby
    Language
baby massage, 117–19, 180
baby yoga, 115
bacterial or yeast infection, 138
baths
  for calming and relief from gas,
    117, 121
  for cooling, 141
  showers, 117, 199–200
bonding. *See also* "lowel": "I'm lonely"
  consequences of inadequate
    attachment, 19, 155
  during feeding, 59
  postpartum depression and, 155, 175
  through responsive caregiving, 3, 18–21
  through smell, 181
bottle-feeding
  allergies and lactose intolerance,
    63, 124–25

bottles and nipples, 63–64
decision to bottle-feed, 57–58
dehydration and thirst, 161, 184, 185
formula types, 62–63, 65–66, 124–25
holds, 59–61
supplement feeding, 53–57
bouncy chairs, 200–1
breast-feeding
  colostrum, 54, 62
  diet and, 122–24, 136, 137
  expressing breast milk, 51–53
  holds, 44–47
  hydration, 161, 183–84
  medication and, 57–58, 139
  milk production, 49–50, 57, 81
  setup and preparation, 43–44
  supplement feeding, 53–57
  switching breasts, 47
burping
  "eh" sound signature and visual cues,
    36–39
  before and during feeding, 47–49,
    94–95
  frequent burping, 48–49, 87, 95–96,
    121, 127
  positions and techniques, 39, 87–92, 95
  prevention of gas accumulation,
    92–94, 121
  upright position, 87, 91, 94, 96–99, 127

Calm the Crying website, 11, 26
car rides
  breaking cycle of upset, 201
  car seat, spinal development and,
    78, 96
  discomfort in car seat, 134–35
  inducement of sleep, 96
  overheating, 185
changing diapers, 85, 131–34
cloth diapers, 129–30

219